A CAPE COD NATIVE RETURNS

YOU <u>CAN</u> GO HOME AGAIN

A CAPE COD NATIVE RETURNS

A CAPE COD NATIVE RETURNS

YOU <u>CAN</u> GO HOME AGAIN

Donald B. Sparrow

Great Oaks Publishing

Eastham, MA

A CAPE COD NATIVE RETURNS

Library of Congress Catalog Card Number 2002095159
Published by the Great Oaks Publishing Co.
Box 1051
Eastham, MA 02642

ISBN 0-9677008-7-6

Dedication

For our beloved hostages to the future:
William, Robert, Perry,
Travis, Alisha and Maya

A CAPE COD NATIVE RETURNS

Table of Contents

Foreword

In the year 2001 my home town, Eastham, celebrated its founding, 350 years ago. As part of the celebration The 350th Anniversary Committee asked this native Eastham resident to write a series of articles for *The Cape Codder*. Good town histories already exist; Alice Lowe's *Nauset on Cape Cod* and Donald Trayser's *Eastham, Massachusetts, 1954* are two; and I cannot pretend to be able to improve on them.

My objectives have been to supply more detail on historical events which were special and/or unique to Eastham's past and to describe my childhood home town. A further objective was to comment on the present Eastham, altered dramatically by three major, post-war events – the explosive growth in summer visitors, the burgeoning year-round retirement population and the coming of the Cape Cod National Seashore in 1961.

The Eastham of today bears little resemblance to the place where I grew up before the post World War II tourist and retirees boom, before the population soared from less than 500 to the present 5,000 year-round residents (20,000 residents and visitors in the summer), and before the Cape Cod National Seashore was established. Now our area is one of the fastest growing and most affluent places in the country. In the "good old days," before the war, our town was not regarded by off-Cape people as a great place to live. Most residents earned a living by putting in long hours of hard physical labor, fishing or farming. Like many of my contemporaries and those preceding us I couldn't wait to escape what seemed to be grim prospects, to leave and seek my fortune on the mainland.

I left in 1939 and, returning 40 years later, I found so many changes that I felt as much a washashore (the term sometimes used to describe one not born on Cape Cod) as the last one over the bridge. But also, I saw the Cape I couldn't wait to leave in a completely different light. I could appreciate the Eastham described so lovingly by Henry Beston (*The Outermost House*) and Wyman Richardson (*The House on Nauset Marsh*), the Atlantic Ocean beaches, Nauset Bay, salt and fresh water ponds, sunrise at Fort Hill, scrub pine forests, and magnificent views where rolling fields interface with the ocean and ponds. These were much the same as in my youth because they were preserved for future generations by the coming of the National Seashore, which brought to a halt housing developments on the 44,000 acres of Outer Cape land the Federal Government has acquired since 1961.

HOW DID YOU TELL TIME WHEN YOU WERE GROWING UP; DID YOU HAVE AN HOUR GLASS?

Shortly after I retired in 1981 I participated in an Eastham Elementary School project with fifth-grade students making a video tape on how people used to live in their town. The teacher introduced me as Don Sparrow to the class of eleven-year-old boys and girls, the video camera's red light appeared and one of the girls posed the first question.

"Now, Don, how did you tell time when you were growing up; did you have an hour glass?"

I had two reactions: first I felt a bit of a shock. It was many years after college before I dared to use the first name in addressing an elder. But then the hour glass question made me wonder exactly what these kids thought about life 100 years ago. How could they possibly know what it was like to live in a town with only 430 people, as few as 4 children in their class, before electricity, automobiles and central heating were commonplace, before airplanes, radio, TV, computers, cellphones and all the other trappings of modern living.

About 20 years ago, with a lot of encouragement from Mr. John Ullman, managing editor of *The Cape Codder*, I began to write a series of articles around one Eastham family, mine. These turned into a book, *Growing Up On Cape Cod*, published in 1999. The more recent 350th

Anniversary articles are the basis for the collection of stories presented here; Eastham people, visitors, and events and how the place has changed over the years. The time span is close to 200 years, 1800s to the present and the material is organized in three sections – happenings before, overlapping, and after 1900.

Nineteenth Century

This was a time when Eastham's population was less than a thousand people and shrinking every year. The rich topsoil that had attracted Eastham's seven first-comer families in 1644 had been farmed out or blown out to sea. The remaining depleted, sandy earth was, in Henry Thoreau's words, "...a substance which gives soil a poor name."

The sea offered the best opportunities for ambitious youngsters. Many sailed the seven seas in clipper ships and whaling vessels. One Eastham sea captain and a relative of mine, Freeman Hatch, still holds the San Francisco to Boston record of 76 days in his vessel, the four-masted *Northern Light*. Eastham's Three Sisters Lighthouses are named after the captain's three nieces. The surrounding water provided other economic opportunities for entrepreneurial Cape Codders:

> as raw material for a major Cape Cod industry, production of salt via solar evaporation of sea water,

> 3,000 miles of cable under the Atlantic terminated in Eastham and connected our country and Europe for the first time, and

> salt water transport in packet ships was an important factor in the success of a revival camp, Millennium Grove, which had as many as 5,000 worshipers on a Sunday in August.

CHAPTER 1

Of English Oaks and Clipper Ships

Growing up on a narrow stretch of sand not more than three miles wide, bordering the Atlantic Ocean, with the nearest land to the east the coast of France 3,000 miles away, it was only natural that many boys in the early days of Eastham took to the sea as a way of life. Teenagers, and even younger, first went to sea as cabin boys or deck hands and worked their way up to command of deep-water vessels when in their twenties. Mrs. Alice Lowe's book, *Nauset on Cape Cod*, gives a number of examples of the maritime careers of Eastham-born men: Ezekiel Doane, born in 1813, started on a fishing vessel when he was eleven years old and at 21 became a ship's master; Clarington Smith, born in 1840, shipped out as cook when eleven years old and was captain of a schooner at 21; and Russel Doane, born in 1801, went to sea at age eleven and first captained ships when he was 26; to name only a few.

One of Eastham's best-known seafaring men, Captain Freeman Hatch, may have been something of a late bloomer. He was all of 33 when he took command of a clipper ship, the *Northern Light*. On his first voyage with her he set a record which still stands. In the words of one of his contemporaries, he was "...a thorough clipper ship captain who never allowed his ship to suffer for want of canvas."

On his record-setting trip he took the *Northern Light* "around the horn," (Cape Horn at the southern tip of South America), from San

Francisco to Boston in 76 days. The story of this epic voyage is well known. Less well known is another of the Captain's exploits, one which had a major impact on the town's landscape. He imported and planted acorns that became the first English Oak trees in Eastham and today the trees and their descendants grace many of Eastham's homesteads.

On one of his voyages after the record-setting trip, he brought back English Oak acorns for his niece, Abbie Chipman Smart. Her husband had emigrated from England

Captain Freeman Hatch

to work at the French Cable Station when it was in Eastham, and the Captain wanted Mr. Smart to have something to remind him of his homeland. The acorns did very well in the Cape Cod soil and the stately trees attaining heights of 50 to 60 feet can be found in numerous Eastham locations, including my own home on Nauset Road. English Oaks lose all their leaves in late fall (unlike other oaks), and in the winter months I find the sight of the clean, bare limbs outlined against the sky, grandiose by day and hauntingly beautiful on a moonlit night.

A number of these oaks are flourishing around the Overlook Inn on Route 6, originally the home of Barnabas Chipman, who married the Captain's sister Sarah. She was the mother of Abbie Smart and one of

The Warner home in the shade of a giant English Oak.

the three Hatch sisters for whom the Three Sisters Lighthouses are named (see next chapter). The Guy Warner house, within the Cape Cod National Seashore boundaries off Nauset Road, where the Captain lived for a while in the late 1800s, also has several of the giant trees. These oaks were huge when I was a boy 70 years ago. Their lower branches extended as much as 40 feet in every direction from a two-foot diameter trunk and their October acorns were bigger than those from any other species of oak. The trees supplied giant missiles for our annual "Acorn Wars" and many of Eastham's English Oaks around our home and the Seashore's Nauset Marsh Trail may have been planted during these far-ranging battles.

Acorns from one of Eastham's first English Oaks.

The Warner house oaks are still standing and still yield extra large acorns. One of my neighbors, Mr. Otto Homburg, a great nephew of Guy Warner, has contributed additional information on how the English Oaks came to Eastham. Lloyd Mayo, a student in Miss Florence Keith's first-grade class in the early 1920s, told him that his teacher had obtained acorns from the oak trees on the Warner property and gave each of her students eight of the acorns with instructions to plant the seeds on their family properties. Judging by the large number of these trees in Eastham, the experiment was a great success. Miss Keith lived in a house across the

THE NORTHERN LIGHT PULLED AHEAD, THE CAPTAIN SIGNALING HE COULDN'T "HOLD HIS HORSE."

street from my present dwelling and I know that she followed her own teachings because the backyard is filled with stately English Oaks. Mr. Homburg also reports that the same species of oak now survive in Pennsylvania and Maryland, where various Warner family members live or have lived.

The story of the Captain's famous voyage has been told often, in the books by Mrs. Alice Lowe and Mr. Donald Trayser, for example, and more recently Noel Beyle has reviewed the episode in an April 1997 issue of *The Cape Codder*. The Captain's vessel, the *Northern Light*, made the record eastward passage in 76 days and 6 hours, beating two New York built clippers, the *Trade Wind* and the *Contest*. The three ships happened to be in the port of San Francisco at the same time and because of the rivalry between Boston and New York shipbuilders a race was proposed. The owner of the *Northern Light*, James Huckins of Boston, promised Captain Hatch a new suit of clothes if he could reach port in the fastest time.

Hatch commanded a beautiful, 180-foot-long four-masted clipper which had been built in South Boston. The *Trade Wind* left port first, on March 10, 1853 (or 1852, the exact date is uncertain), followed by the *Contest* on the 12th and the *Northern Light* on March 13. Captain Hatch passed the *Trade Wind* after a few days out and caught up with the supposedly faster *Contest* as they rounded Cape Horn. The two vessels sailed abreast for several days and then the *Northern Light* pulled ahead, the Captain signaling he couldn't "hold his horse."

On May 29th the *Northern Light* appeared in Boston Harbor under full sail, 76 days out of San Francisco, beating the times of the *Contest* (79 days) and the *Trade Wind* (84 days), into New York. One observer who commented on the arrival stated that "...he brought his vessel across Massachusetts Bay before a fresh easterly breeze, carrying her ringtail, skysails and studding-sails on both sides, alow and aloft, until she was off Boston Light...a superb marine picture." History

The Northern Light. *Captain Hatch sailed from San Francisco to Boston in this vessel, elapsed time, 76 days.*

doesn't record if the Captain got his promised suit but he probably wouldn't have missed it. He went on to a distinguished career, commanding numerous ships that carried cargoes to ports in every part of the world.

CHAPTER 2

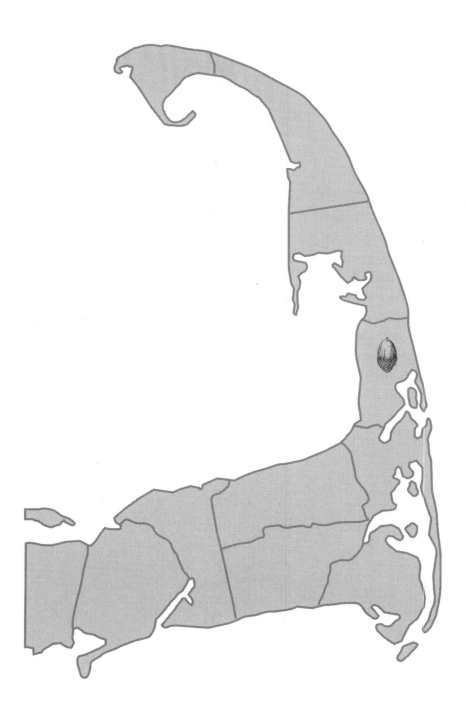

The Three Sisters Lighthouses

Around the time Captain Hatch was setting records for clipper ship operation, one of his Uncles, Henry Y. Hatch, served as light keeper in the three lighthouses on the bluff overlooking Eastham's Nauset Beach on the Atlantic Ocean. The three lights identified the location as Eastham rather than Chatham, which had two lights, or Truro with its one light.

These three lights had always been called the Three Sisters in my memory but I was never clear as to the source of the name until

The Three Sisters Lighthouses

The three Hatch sisters, Sarah, Laura and Abbie.

a friend told me about a tintype photo being offered for sale in a local antique shop. The picture showed three girls in their twenties, arms linked, side by side, looking directly into the camera with an air of confident superiority. The store owners claimed that the picture showed the three Hatch sisters, Abbie, Laura and Sarah, and that the Three Sisters Lighthouses in Eastham had been named after the girls. My great grandmother's maiden name was Elvira Hatch. I bought the picture.

On careful inspection I decided that the girls couldn't be called beautiful – comely, fair, pleasant to look at would be a better description.

The print has been tinted to give their cheeks a slight blush. All three were completely at ease, bearing a trace of a smile, and they looked capable of handling any situation, quietly and competently. Were they related to me and were they the source of the Three Sisters Lighthouse name? I had to know.

The approximate time when the picture was taken was easy to establish. The tintype photograph process was used for only a short time, 1840 – 60. Elvira Hatch was born in 1822 and so could have been a contemporary of Sarah, Laura and Abbie Hatch. But, were they related and how? I called on an Eastham resident, Rachel Hatch, the wife of Freeman Hatch III, whose father, Freeman II, helped oil the first roads in Eastham (see Chapter 8). A genealogy buff, she assured me that Elvira and the three girls shared a common ancestor, Henry Y. Hatch, who was the father of my grandmother Elvira and the sister's uncle and so my grandmother and the three girls were first cousins.

I'm pleased to find that I am related, however remotely, to the three girls. Those Hatch genes have produced some outstanding Eastham people over the years. One of the most notable was Captain Freeman Hatch. Phil Schwind, author, fisherman and renowned raconteur, was another of the Hatch/Eastham notables. John Ullman,

> **A**LL THREE WERE COMPLETELY AT EASE, BEARING A TRACE OF A SMILE, AND THEY LOOKED CAPABLE OF HANDLING ANY SITUATION, QUIETLY AND COMPETENTLY.

for many years the distinguished managing editor of *The Cape Codder* and owner Malcolm Hobbs' right-hand man, has the distinction of being the issue of two Hatch lines. His father, a Hatch descendent, was married to a Miss Edna Hatch. When I observed that this certainly explained a lot of things he only chuckled and commented, "fools and geniuses."

The second part of my quest, the lighthouse connection, has been more difficult. None of my Eastham sources could confirm the story and none of the history books on Eastham had helped. I heard that the Three Sisters' log had been given to a local doctor and his heirs might be in Miami. This too proved to be a dry well. I was on the point of ascribing the story to an antique dealer's creative imagination when I chanced upon a 1853 deed with the opening words,

"I, Henry Y. Hatch, Light Keeper of Eastham..."

"Eureka, the loop has been closed," I thought. Further research had been fruitless, until a friend, Kate Alpert (Moore), retired last year and moved back to her home town. The Moores lived next to Mr. John

Smart, a French Cable Station employee whose wife was a daughter of Sarah Hatch Chipman, sister to Laura and Abbie. One of Kate's childhood memories is of Mr. Smart, on a number of occasions, telling her folks that Eastham's three sisters lighthouses were named for his wife's mother and two aunts. – Q.E.D. Until information to the contrary is found, in my book the Three Sisters Lighthouses were named after the indomitable trio: Abbie, Laura and Sarah.

CHAPTER 3

Sea Water, Sunshine, and Salt[1]

*T*he sea provided an opportunity for many like Captain Hatch to escape from the hard work of scratching a living from Cape Cod's sandy soil, by roaming the world in clipper ships and whaling vessels. For a time in the 1800s the sea supplied another source of revenue for enterprising Cape Codders, producing salt via solar evaporation of salt water. Sunshine and salt water, now the Cape's major attractions for tourists and retirees, were also the raw materials for an industry which played an important role in its economy about 150 years ago. In 1837, the peak year of salt production, Cape Codders produced 662,000 bushels of salt, (equivalent to 26,480 tons), in 658 saltworks in towns from Sandwich to Provincetown.

The income from the sale of salt had a considerable impact on Cape Cod's economy. Investors could count on a return of at least 25 percent on their money. After a Federal

---

[1] The above is abstracted from *The Saltworks of Historic Cape Cod*, Parnassus Imprints. Orleans, Massachusetts, 1993 by William P. Quinn. Bill is one of the authors of this article and the pictures were also taken from Bill's book.

tariff was put on salt in the early 1800s, it sold for $19 per ton and the 26,680 tons produced in 1837 would have yielded $500,000. A sizeable sum at a time when the total revenues of the United States Government amounted to only $30 million.

Development of the first successful solar-evaporation saltworks on Cape Cod is credited to a Captain John Sears of Dennis. His first works, at Dennis' Quivet Neck on Sesuit Harbor, yielded only eight bushels of salt in its first year, 1776. Over the next 20 years he and others introduced numerous improvements and by the end of the 1700s salt production started to expand rapidly all over the Cape. Dubbed "Sleepy John" in his early years because of his habit of sitting in silence for long periods of time, impervious to all conversational approaches, Captain Sears acquired the nickname "Salt John" after the success of his developments.

Sea water contains about 2.7 percent salt (sodium chloride) and so the Cape is surrounded by millions of tons of the compound. The trick is to remove the water in order to recover the dry salt. The Cape salt-works, as developed and refined by "Salt" John Sears and others, used banks of wooden trays fitted with removable covers which were taken off during good weather and put back on at night or when rain fell. The time needed to concentrate the water to the point that salt crystals formed varies depending on temperature and other weather conditions, but on Cape Cod it generally took three to six days.

Windmill-powered pumps lifted the sea water (350 gallons of sea water gave one bushel or 80 pounds of salt) to the top level of vats and as the water evaporated the fluid was transferred to a succession of lower tanks. In the highest, or "water" tanks, suspended solids such as silt, sea-weed and marine organisms settled to the bottom. This clarified sea water was then allowed to flow to the "pickle" vats where calcium salts, mainly limestone, precipitated and collected at the vat bottoms.

When a saline film of "pellicle" began to form on its surface, the liq-uid was drawn to the "salt" vats, where salt crystals grew and collected on the tank's floor. Finally, the concentrated solution, called lye or bit-

Saltworks in South Yarmouth with the covers off and vats exposed (middle right of picture).

tern, was withdrawn and the salt crystals removed and sent to the drying room.

The bittern contained other salts that could be recovered when cooled in the winter months. To avoid confusion, the initial salt recovered (sodium chloride), was also known as marine salt. As the bittern cooled and the temperature dropped, crystals of Glaubers Salt (hydrated sodium sulfate) appeared. At an appropriate time the liquid was decanted from the Glaubers Salt crystals and additional crystals of another chemical grew, Epsom salts or magnesium sulfate. These latter two substances had considerable commercial value and were harvested in the more technically advanced saltworks. For example, when marine salt sold for $19 per ton in the early 1800s, a ton of Glaubers Salt was worth $130.

Finally, the Epsom salts could be processed further to produce another chemical of value. This was accomplished by redissolving the Epsom salt, treating the brine with a water extract of wood ashes and heating the mixture. The resulting reaction gave a heavy, precipitate of magnesium hydroxide, commonly known as Magnesia, which was in great demand in the medical profession.

Solids collected in the first- and second-stage tanks (water and pickle vats) were used as fertilizer, the limestone content being particularly desirable on the acidic Cape soil. The main product, marine salt from the third stage, salt vat, was used for salting fish, and frequently fish-drying racks and saltworks were located side by side. Other food preservation applications and curing hides offered additional markets and the purest product went to table salt. The three other saltworks products – Glaubers Salt, Epsom salts, and Magnesia – went to the medical profession, primarily to be used as laxatives.

The basic saltworks unit was a wooden vat ten feet wide, ten to sixteen feet long, and eight to twelve inches deep. Each vat had a cover which was put in place every night and during the day in rainy or foggy conditions. Some of the covers moved on wooden or iron rollers while others were constructed in cantilevered pairs and pivoted on a central post (crane covers).

Most of the installations were small; ten to twenty thousand square feet was typical. This seemed to be a size that could be operated by a single family comprised of "mom and pop" and numerous children, typical of families in those days. A sudden shower called for fast help from the entire family and the sound generated by roller covers being moved has been compared to the rumble of distant thunder.

The supply of local lumber wasn't adequate to keep up with demand during the period of saltworks expansion after 1800. Large quantities of Maine lumber – spruce, hemlock and pine – were imported. Boards needed to be the best quality, straight and free of knots so as to prepare water-tight tanks. Pipes for carrying water to the windmill and to the vats were generally made by hollowing a log by cutting or burning out its center.

Sea water contains other valuable materials, notably gold, but in such low concentrations that recovery is not practical. The amount of this precious metal in the ocean water ranges from five to 300 parts per 100 million. By one estimate the earth's sea water contains ten billion tons of gold, a figure which has excited great interest in recovery processes. To date, all of them have been fraudulent. One of the most successful, or outrageous, of the scams was the Lubec Klondike Caper. In 1898, two men, Charles Fisher and the Reverend Prescott Jernegan, doing business as the "Electrolytic Marine Salts Company," set up machinery to extract gold from sea water in Lubec, Maine. Investors were invited to come to Lubec to view the process and to buy stock in the company. Encouraged by bits of gold dust supposedly produced by their equipment, visitors poured money into the venture. Over $9,000,000 (in 1898 dollars), was invested by the gullible before the newspapers began to ask questions and the pair, Fisher and the "Reverend" Jernegan, disappeared from the little Maine town.

Salt production via solar evaporation on Cape Cod expanded rapidly in the early 1800s, peaked in 1837, and then declined just as rapidly. By 1845, the 1937 output of over 600,000 bushels had been reduced by 50 percent and to less than 100,000 bushels in 1865. The end came in 1888 when Yarmouth's last plant shut down. Many factors contributed to its downfall. The Federal Government gradually reduced its tariff protection starting in 1839. Large salt mines were exploited in New York State, and the opening of the Erie Canal in 1825 and the extension of railroad lines made this salt available at low cost all over the East Coast; the local fishing industry faced stiffer competition from the much larger Boston and Gloucester ports and Maine lumber became more costly.

As their economic viability declined, the saltwork structures began to shut down and the thrifty Cape Codders used the good Maine lumber for shed, barn and house construction. Carpenters cursed it because the salt-saturated wood dulled and corroded their tools. Also, it would not hold paint and the boards which had been steeped in salt brine for many years exuded salt for a long time. With the passage of time, homes constructed of saltworks boards tended to sway in a high wind. Nails rusted away quickly, leaving rust spots in place of solid iron fasteners. These rust spots are among the few traces of the saltworks in Eastham.

Salt is still produced via solar evaporation in various places around the world where climate, rainfall and coastal geography are favorable.

Travelers to San Francisco pass over hundreds of acres of salt-producing ponds as their plane comes in for a landing. Most of this is used on roads for melting snow and ice. Recently, solar salt producers in Europe have been offering a gourmet sea salt called sel de fleur (France), or flor de sal (Portugal), which is produced by skimming off the first, saline film of pellicle which appears as salt starts to crystallize. The author of a recent *Atlantic Monthly* article describes it as a dazzling white, crystalline substance, "so sweet, so creamy, you won't believe it." And, it sells in Boston markets for thirty dollars a pound.

From the patio in front of the Cape Cod National Seashore Visitors Center in Eastham, one has a good view of the site of a small saltworks installation, on the bank to the right of the inlet to Salt Pond. The vats were positioned on a 20 foot bluff adjacent to the inlet. A windmill-powered pump supplied salt water to the first tanks. The land slopes gradually to sea level over thirty to forty feet to the South where the

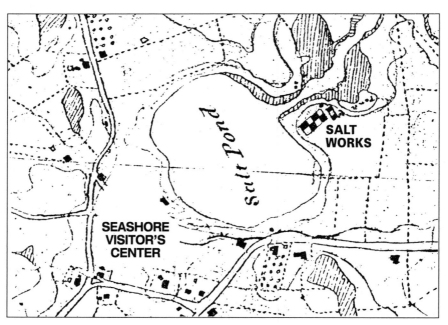

Saltworks in Eastham located on the western shore of Salt Pond,
Cape Cod National Seashore Visitor's Center and Nauset Road to the left.

final, "bittern" tanks were located – a picture book saltworks installation. After the facility no longer operated, the land was used for farming, then the 11th hole of Cedar Banks golf course, (see Chapter 20) and finally preserved in its natural state by the establishment of the National Seashore.

The site would be an ideal spot for a salt-from-sea-water demonstration plant, a major tourist attraction. A ten thousand square foot salt works might produce 136,000 lbs of product per summer season. While only ten percent of this would be recovered as gourmet salt, the annual dollar sales from 13,600 lbs of Cape Cod National Seashore fleur de sel could be as much as $400,000 at the Boston sales price.

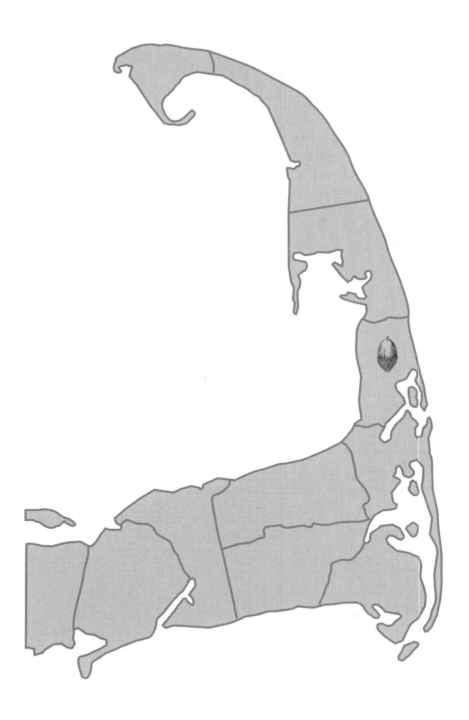

CHAPTER 4

Eastham's French Cable Station

*T*he sea offered attractive commercial opportunities for Cape Codders – world wide trade in sailing vessels, fishing, whaling, and salt recovery from sea water – but it also imposed a barrier to communication with the rest of the world. This changed forever when the first underwater cable connected Cape Cod on the East Coast of the United States and Europe in 1879. Delivery time for letters between Europe and the North American continent, a matter of weeks when sailing vessels carried the mail, was reduced to minutes. This became the only means of fast exchange of business, diplomatic, and personal information between the United States and Europe until wireless signals were beamed across the Atlantic Ocean by Marconi in the early 1900s. Marconi and the cable companies came to outer Cape Cod for their first United States contacts for the same reason – it provided the shortest, great circle distance for cable or wireless from Europe to the United States.

In the middle 1860s the French firm, Compagnie Francaise des Cables Telegraphiques, laid 2,200 miles of cable from Brest in France to the St. Pierre and Miquelon Islands just off the coast of Newfoundland. Their first United States connection was an underwater cable to Duxbury, Massachusetts, in 1869, but this line experienced technical difficulties and they sold to the Anglo-American Telegraph Co. four years later.

In 1879 the French company employed the English steamer *Faraday* to put down 820 miles of cable from the St. Pierre and Miquelon Islands to Cape Cod and it arrived in Eastham waters on November 15. The *Faraday* anchored about one mile off what is now Nauset Light Beach. A group of Eastham men rowed out to greet the crew and assist in the cable landing but inclement weather forced postponement of the great event to the following day. Miss Matilda Smart, a life-long Eastham resident and daughter of a cable employee, discussed the ensuing events in tape recordings of "Eastham Celebrities" by Colonel Clark. By Miss Smart's account,

> A section of the cable was then brought in, on a towed raft, in late afternoon and touched shore, "amid the fury of guns and the cheers of the multitude." Flags of France, America and England flew on the *Faraday*; more than a thousand people watched from shore, including directors of the cable company brought from Boston by special train. The following day, Monday, November 17, 1879, at midday the splice between the land and the *Faraday* cable ends was made and the first messages sent, an exchange of greetings between company officials in France and America.

Equipment was set up in the basement of the Nauset light keepers house pending completion of a permanent Cable Station structure. Twelve operators came from abroad, one from Belgium and the rest from England and Scotland, no one from France. The Cable Station building was completed two weeks after the marine and on-land cables had been spliced. It held business equipment, a few accommodations for staff

Old French Cable Station – A well-remembered building in North Eastham near the Nauset lights. It housed the land terminus of the French cable between 1879 and 1891. One of the lights shows faintly at the left of the station.

members, and a large space for social gatherings. The town put in an arrow-straight road, now Cable Road, from Nauset Road east to Lighthouse Beach and the new Cable Station.

Miss Smart's father, John Smart, worked for the French Cable Company in its New York office. A native of Bristol, England, he had moved to the New York office and then came to Eastham when the French cable arrived here. An 1881 picture of the crew includes the young John Smart. He married Miss Sarah Chipman, whose mother was one of the three sisters for whom the three lighthouses were named. John and Sarah made their home in the old Eastham Town Hall on what is now Route 6 across from the Seashore Visitors Center. John bought it in 1913 and named it "The Wellington" after the two-masted schooner *J. V. Wellington*. His father-in-law, Captain Barnabas Chipman, was the owner and Master of this vessel. Matilda never married and lived in the house until her death in the mid 1970s.

French Cable Station Crew – An 1881 photograph showing the crew of the cable station. Front row, left to right: C. Albert Ronne, Mr. Self, A. F. "Fred" Toovey, Superintendent Charles Marsily, H. G. Wilson, George S. Hall ,and Nathan A. Gill, keeper of the Nauset lights; rear row, left to right, Mr. Quinn, James D. B. Stuart, George Williams, Everett G. Dill, and John H. Smart.

Miss Smart reported that finding lodging was a problem and her quote of the locals' characterization of the group as "foreigners" may indicate some resentment of these overseas invaders. Problems with the location plagued the company and its staff. Workers did not have the means of transportation for school children and the town didn't provide any. The nearest neighbors, stores and churches were at some distance and winter storms coming off the Atlantic Ocean made life unpleasant for the operators and their families.

After nine years the company built a new cable station near the Orleans Town Cove, brought the cable overland from North Eastham and then under the Cove and transferred operations to the more populous town. John Smart continued to work for the cable company, in its new office at Orleans. Three employees had built houses in Eastham and these were moved to Orleans and are occupied today. One of them is the home of the Beth Bishop Shop.

In 1893 the cable company sold the Eastham building to a Fairhaven man who tried to run a resort hotel there, with limited success. After several years a fire totally destroyed the structure and put an end to the business. No trace of the building remains. The site is probably under water now in view of the three-foot-per-year beach erosion rate.

When the station building was sold, the company built a small hut to serve as a cable connecting point. The hut housed the cable connection until the Germans invaded and occupied France in 1940. At that time communication over the line ceased and the building was boarded up. Over the years it has gone through a number of ownerships and structural modifications but is still standing on its original site and is now listed on the National Register of Historic Places. The only other evidence of the Eastham installation was, when I was young, a two to three inch diameter cable protruding from the sand dunes at Lighthouse Beach and leading down to the ocean's edge. Now even this is gone, a victim of the encroaching Atlantic or souvenir hunters, or both.

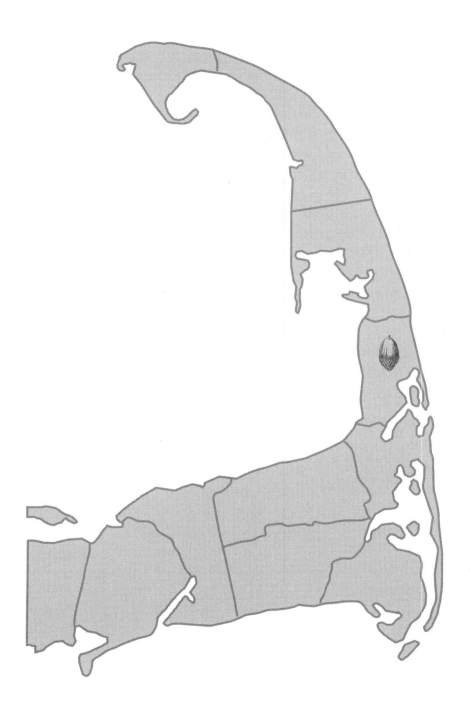

CHAPTER 5

Prayer and Picnic Days[1]

Transport by sailing vessels also played an important role in religious life in Eastham in the 1800s. Millennium Grove, a Methodist revival camp in Eastham, attracted thousands of worshipers throughout the middle of the 19th century, many of whom arrived by sea. The camp was in North Eastham, across from the present-day Council on Aging Thrift Shop on Massasoit Road.

It evolved from a series of Methodist revival meetings held in Wellfleet, Truro, and then in Eastham from 1819 to 1826. In 1828, the Eastham revival site was purchased by an association formed for that purpose. The level, ten-acre lot was covered with oaks and pines and situated near Cape Cod Bay, where steamboats and other vessels might land their passengers and was ideally suited to its purpose.

A location close to water transportation was important because there was no railroad,

---

[1] In preparing the above I borrowed liberally from: *Eastham, Massachusetts 1651 - 1951*, Donald G. Trayser, The Eastham Tercentenary Committee, 1951, and *Comprehensive History of Eastham, Wellfleet and Orleans*, Rev. Enoch Pratt, W. S. Fisher and Co., Yarmouth, 1844.

roads were poorly developed, and people came not only from Eastham, but the rest of the Cape, New England, and even further away to

Landing at Eastham for the camp meeting.

attend the meetings. Packets from Cape towns as well as Plymouth and Boston delivered passengers to Eastham's West Shore, now known as Campground Landing, then they waded ashore and walked almost a mile to Camp. When the famous Boston paddle-wheel steamer, *Naushon*, made one of its frequent runs to West Shore, passengers were ferried to shallow water in small boats, transferred to horse and cart for the ride to dry land, and then had to walk the sandy mile to Camp.

A Boston artist made the trip in 1852 and recorded his impressions as follows:

> From the paddle-wheel steamer, *Naushon*, he stepped into a small boat, roomy enough for 20 into which 67 passengers were crammed. Away it ran for shore until a horse-drawn pillbox loomed up. Passengers transferred again, "stowed like bales of cotton," and then away, helter-skelter, the horses stumbling, water splashing around us, some quarter miles through the receding tide...drenching the nether portions of our persons.

Once in camp, the congregation was housed in tents arranged to form a circle in which they slept, cooked and took their meals. A large house had been erected for the accommodation of the ministers.

Judging from the sketch by the Boston artist, the two-story structure had a platform from which the ministers addressed the crowds. Creature comforts were minimal. The guest speakers slept on straw spread on the floor of their house and the congregation sat on raised planks with no back support while listening to the sermons. The name, Millennium Grove, didn't have a connection with the year 2000, but rather because the name suggests the character of the blessings received. By one definition in *Webster's*

Prayer meeting in a tent.

Dictionary it is "a period of general righteousness and happiness, especially in the future."

Revival meetings were held for one week, usually in August, beginning on Tuesday and continuing through the following Monday. Sunday

Exhortation and preaching at the camp meeting at Eastham.

was naturally the well attended day, when an estimated 5,000 of the faithful may have been present. They were serious about their observance of their faith. According to Enoch Pratt's book, "The exercises are, three sermons delivered from the stand each day, prayer and exhortatory meetings in the center of the camp, and in the tents during intermission." The drawing of a Preacher, "exhorting," indicates that attention of the audience may have flagged occasionally.

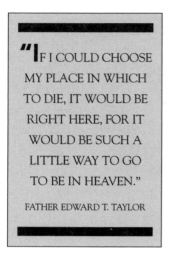

"IF I COULD CHOOSE MY PLACE IN WHICH TO DIE, IT WOULD BE RIGHT HERE, FOR IT WOULD BE SUCH A LITTLE WAY TO GO TO BE IN HEAVEN."

FATHER EDWARD T. TAYLOR

Preachers came from the ranks of the leading Methodist ministers of the day. One of the more prominent, Father Edward T. Taylor, long-term pastor of Seaman's Bethel in Boston, attended every Eastham meeting from first to last. As evidence of his dedication to Millennium Grove, he once remarked, "If I could choose my place in which to die, it would be right here, for it would be such a little way to go to be in heaven."

Published reports on Millennium Grove deal lightly with the subject of living conditions in the Camp during the week-long sessions. The only source of water was a single wooden pump with one man to operate it. People queued up at the pump with pails, pitchers and bowls, waiting their turn to be served. One can only speculate on sanitation matters. Bathing probably was accomplished in the Bay or one of Eastham's many freshwater ponds. Each tent must have had its own latrine and garbage was thrown into pits and covered with sand.

Families came for the week with huge hampers of food, supplemented by readily available lobster, shellfish and fish. One writer reported seeing great piles of oyster, clam and lobster shells outside each tent. Anyone who visited the Eastham Sanitary Landfill in the days when the garbage was piled up on a hot August day, prior to burial, can imagine the vapors rising from the Camp at the end of a revival week.

The week was not all sermons and exhortations. Thoreau called it a combination of prayer meeting and picnic. Trayser reported that the ever-present Father Taylor was once dispatched to quiet a happy band who continued to sing songs of praise. Soon his powerful voice was heard leading the band with great gusto. "We'll feed on milk and honey..." Enoch Pratt's history of Eastham has some gentle, but unmistakable references to the problems generated by a week-long assembly of people in a vacation mood. "The meetings brought together very large numbers of not only Methodists, but other societies.

"The strictest regulations have been found necessary to preserve that order and attention that such a meeting demands." In another paragraph he writes, " – large numbers were hopefully converted and many backsliders reclaimed; but recently this does not seem to be the happy result, and the same is true of other protracted meetings." One of Eastham's grand dames and a sharp observer of the passing parade has commented of the later years of Millennium Grove, "More souls were created than saved."

Enthusiasm for the revival meetings waned in the 1850s and the extension of the railroad to Yarmouth put the finishing touches on Eastham's meeting place. The meetings moved to Yarmouth and Millennium Grove was abandoned in 1863. Now a few private dwellings occupy the area and the only reminder of the prayer and picnic days is the West Shore beach called Campground Landing.

Turn of the Century

As the nineteenth century merged into the twentieth, making a living on Cape Cod became increasingly difficult and Eastham's population continued to decline. This section provides a "snapshot" of Eastham based on the 1900 town report – the state of the economy and how the people dealt with issues such as school, welfare and public safety.

It also describes the daily lives of Eastham residents in the early days of the twentieth century,

> the two town shopping area, George Clark's and Sam Brackett's stores, how they also served as the town's social centers and their fate as the automobile replaced horse-drawn vehicles,

> how Eastham served as a guinea pig in early experiments on paving dirt roads,

> an oration by the town's water supply, composed by a deaf-mute school boy, and

> the rigors of weir fishing and quahoging as a way of life.

CHAPTER 6

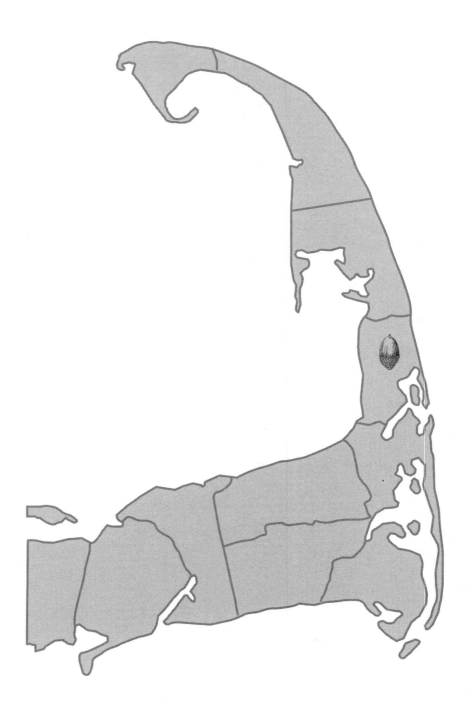

A Snapshot of Eastham One Hundred Years Ago

Eastham's 350th Anniversary celebration combined with the high degree of public interest in this millennium year led me to wonder what Eastham was like 100 years ago. Eastham's Town Reports proved to be a mother lode of facts about the times, population, the economy, schools, public safety provisions, the Public Library and welfare expenses.

POPULATION

Eastham's population, like that of the rest of Cape Cod, declined steadily from the middle 1800s to the 1920s. Close to 1,000 in 1830, the number of residents had declined to 500 by 1900 and bottomed out at 420 in 1920. The slight increases in 1930 and 1940 are, I believe, a result of the 1930's Great Depression. There were few opportunities for employment off Cape. In addition, a number of family heads were unable to find work in the cities and moved the family back to a place where they could survive by fishing, digging quahogs, growing vegetables and keeping a flock of chickens.

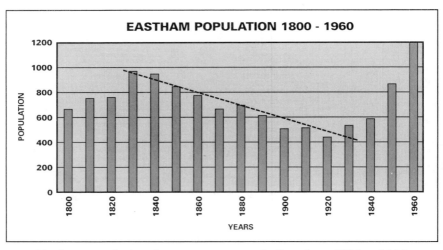

Eastham population, 3 percent per year decline, from 1830 to 1930.

The rate of decline was a steady one percent per year while the population of the entire state of Massachusetts was increasing by an average of two percent annually. Eastham was losing an average of three percent of its natural growth every year. A three percent per year decrease may not seem like much, but it translates to about 15 people each year in the early 1920s and these were usually the more aggressive, more enterprising individuals – the "best and the brightest." This loss had to have a debilitating effect on the succeeding generations. I can say this because my immediate ancestors stayed in Eastham, in many cases the less energetic members of the family. The "brain drain" may have had a negative impact on the family line as illustrated in my discussion of welfare costs.

THE ECONOMY

Fishing, shellfishing and farming were the mainstays of Eastham's 1900 economy. The Board of Selectmen's town assessment listed 169 houses, 137 horses, 125 cows and 8,043 fowl. Almost every household had a cow, a horse and a flock of chickens. Asparagus and turnips were the major farm crops, while fish and shellfish were harvested from the Bay waters of Cape Cod by means of weir or trap fishing, digging clams

Eastham's one room schoolhouse in 1897.

or scratching for quahogs. In addition, most of the able-bodied men in town worked on the roads. In 1900, over 150 men were paid for their snow removal or road maintenance services. Subsequent chapters will describe how people made a living in these various ways.

SCHOOLS

The *1900 Town Report* tells us that each of the three one-room schoolhouses in Eastham had about 25 students, grades one through eight, and one teacher for each school. Eastham's Historical Society Museum building, opposite the Seashore Park Visitor's Center, is the school shown in the 1897 picture of the schoolchildren posed in front of the building. The three separate buildings were combined at the central location in 1905 and remained there until the school moved to a new building in 1936.

The 1897 picture is special to me for another reason – three of the 17 students are family, my father and two of his sisters. Dan (age nine) is second from the left, Rosie (eleven) ninth from the left, and Marion (fourteen) fourth from the right. A fourth sibling, 13 years old at the time, Uncle Frank, was absent or had already dropped out, and a fifth,

Uncle Rob, was 5 years old and slated to start school the following year. The Sparrow clan comprised over 25 percent of that school's population at one time.

Reading these early town reports, I was pleased to find that the names of my father and his siblings appeared frequently on the honor roll – pleased until I found that inclusion in the honor roll depended upon a lack of absences and tardiness, not intellectual attainment. To emphasize the importance of promptness, the principal wrote, "The habit of punctuality is too valuable to be trifled with. Let the cooperation of the home and school be brought to bear upon this thief of opportunity – this evil upon the children."

The school principal was also much concerned about the problem of finding qualified teachers for "mixed" schools. This term confused me (did he mean racially mixed or boys and girls together?) until I realized he was referring to the problem of one teacher handling students aged six to fifteen in one room.

There were two or three classes per teacher when I was a student there in the 1920s and '30s. I found more than one class per room to be advantageous. Listening to everything going on, I ended the year with a good grasp on the content of all three classes and, as a result, received frequent double promotions.

Not many of those who stayed the course in grammar school went on to high school. Only nine Eastham children were enrolled in Orleans High in 1900. This was the first year that the Eastham students were provided with transportation to high school. They were carried in a horse-drawn wagon called a barge. Thinking that the word barge always referred to a water-borne vessel, I looked up the term in the *Random House Dictionary of the English Language* and was pleased to find "In New England, a large four wheel coach with two seats."

As in my time at Orleans High in the 1930s, Eastham students were regarded with some reservations. The principal in his 1900 report says, "The pupils in attendance at the Orleans High from the town of Eastham <u>seem</u> to have had adequate preparation – they have <u>thus far</u>

Orleans High School, early 1900s.

maintained a high standard in scholarship and deportment, (emphasis added by author). The reservations about Eastham students lasted a long time. In 1933, my freshman year at Orleans, when a friend and I scored 100 in our first math test, the teachers conducted an investigation, thinking that the Eastham students <u>must</u> have cheated.

PUBLIC SAFETY

Expenditures for public safety were not major budget items in 1900. The constable received $10 a year and appointed fire wardens were paid only on the basis of specific actions in attending to fires. One warden was paid $39 for an apparently serious fire and another got $1.50 for a brush fire. Fires caused by the coal-burning railroad engines were a serious concern. The New York, New Haven and Hartford Railroad Company, (N.Y., N.H. & H. R.R. Co.), was billed for the cost of taking care of numerous fires each year. In one apparently dry year the town report records 18 railroad-caused fires. A listing of the firefighting equipment available to the volunteers gives some clues as to the fires they

Eastham Library, about 1900.

were capable of dealing with. In 1921, for example, the town owned six extinguishers, six Marshfield cans, twelve wire brooms, and twenty-four short-handled shovels. Obviously, brush fires were their target.

The nearest fire engine was in Orleans, until 1947 when the first Eastham fire equipment was purchased. Prior to that, by the time the Orleans fire truck made it to Eastham, a serious fire such as a blazing house could only be controlled and confined to the site. In the 1930s, when I was a child, a horn mounted on a 25-foot tower beside the Town Hall signaled the location of fires. Three long and one short blast, for example, might mean a fire in the Nauset region and the volunteers rushed to the area to try to contain it until the Orleans fire truck made it to Eastham.

THE PUBLIC LIBRARY

In 1898 Eastham's Public Library had just moved into its new quarters on Samoset Road from its former location in George Clark's store, across from the railroad station. The Village Improvement Society had built it in 1897 and rented it to the Library for "a nominal sum" each year. In 1903 the Society sold it to the town for the token sum of one dollar. The picture was taken before the town installed a basement shortly after its purchase. The windows are placed substantially higher than in a private dwelling on orders from a Captain Savage, a Library Trustee and Chairman of the Building Committee, "so that the reader's attention would not be distracted by anything outside."

Taxpayer support for the library was not exactly lavish in the early days. The 1900 Town Meeting appropriated $25 and also voted to transfer $56.20 from the refunded dog tax to the library. Then, as now, the state collected the dog tax and then refunded a portion to the individual towns. Every year, and to this day, one hundred years later, one of the first articles on the Town Meeting Warrant calls for the assignment of the refunded dog tax to the library. When I was on the Library Board of Trustees, a Town Meeting member tried to have the money transferred to another Town department. The Trustees fought for (and won) the money even though it represented less than two percent of the library's annual budget.

> THE WINDOWS ARE PLACED SUBSTANTIALLY HIGHER THAN IN A PRIVATE DWELLING "SO THAT THE READER'S ATTENTION WOULD NOT BE DISTRACTED BY ANYTHING OUTSIDE."

From 1900 on, the Library managed to operate with its $25 a year Town appropriation (plus the refunded dog tax) for many years. The annual interest from a $14,000 bequest by Mr. Robert Billings helped a lot. The Billings fund annual interest paid a significant part of the total budget until the 1930s when the Town Meetings began to consider annual increases.

The Billings bequest created some problems, or opportunities, for Mr. George Dill, the town clerk at the time. The first three years he charged the town amounts ranging from $4.50 to $15.60 for carfare, labor and expenses to travel to Boston to collect the twice yearly interest on the Billings money. After 1906, town officials learned that the bank book could be mailed to the New England Trust Co. and a check returned for the amount of the interest.

POOR EXPENSES

Until 1905, the Eastham Town Reports listed all the details of the "poor expenses." The Sparrow name was embarrassingly abundant in the listings of those citizens on welfare from 1886 to 1905, perhaps a result of the loss of the "best and brightest." The less energetic of our ancestors, Caleb, Louisa, Elvira, and Catherine Sparrow, appeared just about every year in the welfare rolls. Expenses included board, supplies, medicine and attendance, wearing apparel and even tobacco. Caleb's name appeared most frequently and he received as much as $200 a year, this at a time when the total town operating budget was only $4,000. He disappeared from the Town Report in 1905 when an item showed $42.32 as the cost of transporting Caleb Sparrow to Tewksbury (the location of the state poor farm).

Other poor expenses included the cost of transport of shipwrecked sailors off Cape. On March 2, 1900, Eastham paid the New York, New Haven and Hartford Railroad Company (N.Y., N.H. & H. R.R. Co.) to transport 18 of such unfortunates from North Eastham to Boston. Curious about the details on the shipwreck, I asked the Orleans expert on things maritime, Bill Quinn, if he could find any information. He didn't disappoint me. The United States Life Saving Service Reports, 1900, tells us that the fishing schooner Mondago out of Gloucester stranded on Nauset Beach shortly after midnight on March 1, 1900. Surfmen from the Nauset Lifesaving Station assisted the crew to get to shore, but the vessel and cargo were a total loss. This was not an uncommon occurrence. The Town Reports list funds laid out to transport shipwrecked sailors every year in the early 1900s.

CHAPTER 7

The Center of Town

Motorists crossing the bike trail while driving west on Samoset Road see nothing to indicate that they are passing an historic spot. From 1871 to the mid-1920s, this was one of two social and economic centers of Eastham, the location of the railroad station and George Clark's store. Sam Brackett's store (now the Council on Aging Thrift Shop) and the nearby North Eastham railroad depot became the other Eastham social and economic center. The bike trail follows the old railroad right-of-way and the Eastham station, or Depot, was at the southeast corner of the Samoset Road and bike trail intersection. The station was built in 1870, the year the rail tracks were extended from Orleans to Wellfleet, by the Cape Cod Railway Co., which became the Old Colony Railway in 1873 and then the New Haven Railway in 1893 (the full name was the New York, New Haven and Hartford Railroad or N.Y., N.H. & H. R.R.).

The station building itself held a waiting room, a freight storage area and a small office for the station master. The last person to hold this position, and the one I remember, was

N.Y., N.H. & H. R.R. Company Depot in Eastham at the turn of the century.

Cavalier Robbins. He was a short, wiry man with a thatch of pure white hair and a matching moustache. Despite his slight frame, he easily wrestled the huge steamer trunks accompanying some of the passengers off the train and to the waiting carts.

Beside the track, on the other side of Samoset Road, was a freight loading platform and a two-story building with side sheds for storage of grain, coal, building products and other commodity shipments. Next to it was a water tower, twenty feet in diameter and fifteen feet high, standing on four legs about ten feet high and equipped with a swing pipe to transfer water to the steam locomotives. At one point a second water tower existed, but this had been dismantled by the 1920s. The rail line was single tracked, with a siding at each station to store rail cars for unloading and reloading, and to allow trains heading the opposite direction to pass. Across the tracks (now across the bike trail) was Clark's general merchandise store. In addition to selling a wide range of products – hardware, farm equipment, groceries, sugar, flour and

Another view of Eastham's Depot, showing storage sheds and water tank, about 1915.

other household staples – the store housed the Town Library from 1878 to 1898, and the Eastham Post Office until the store burned in 1924. The owner, George Clark, also served as Postmaster, and family members served terms as library trustees and librarian.

In Eastham, as all across the United States, the extension of rail transport through the town center and beyond had an enormous impact on the town and townspeople. Goods which formerly had to be shipped in by packet boat or horse cart were delivered in quantity at lower cost and without regard for the weather. Just about everyone in town found reason to come to the depot: dairy farmers, asparagus and turnip growers, clamdiggers, quahoggers and fishermen to ship their produce to market and to shop for supplies; housewives to do their weekly shopping; young boys to put pennies on the tracks so the train could press them to half dollar size; and teenagers to socialize and get the mail. In Col. Clark's 1963 tape on "Eastham Celebrities," Ralph Chase described the scene as follows:

The town center, George Clark's store with Depot across the tracks and water tank to the left.

Well, in those days one of the biggest attractions was to go to the Eastham railroad station and see the evening train come in. It would arrive at Eastham at 7:30 p.m., about four hours after leaving Boston. Most of the people, young and old, would gather at George Clark's store, which was directly across the tracks from the station. And when the train whistled up the line, in the vicinity of Bill Nickerson's, they would all rush out of the store to the station to see who came in on the train, to take a look at the incoming express and to see if anyone was having any liquor come in.

I can't explain the liquor reference except to theorize that the observation came from Prohibition times, when the locals were remarkably casual about the 18th Amendment to the Constitution. Mr. Chase concludes by saying,

And it was also quite an attraction for the young people, as it gave many a young blade the opportunity to walk his best girl home, a far cry from today's modern techniques of fraternizing.

To this I add, Amen.

The possibility of a four-hour journey to Boston opened new worlds to Eastham residents, accustomed to a full day or more stage coach ride to the capital city. To promote rail travel, the railroad company offered free tickets to Boston to railroad company stockholders to its annual meeting in Boston. This usually came two days before Thanksgiving and the company ran special trains to accommodate those taking advantage of the opportunity to shop and visit relatives in Boston. This was the first, and in some cases, the only time many ever left the Cape. One story told in my youth, perhaps apocryphal, had one early 1900s farmer taking a day trip to Boston and spending the whole time inspecting the many shops and other attractions in South Station. Upon his return he told his friends about the splendors of Boston, but was puzzled by one thing. He had never realized that the city was totally covered by one roof.

> IT WAS ALSO QUITE AN ATTRACTION FOR THE YOUNG PEOPLE, AS IT GAVE MANY A YOUNG BLADE THE OPPORTUNITY TO WALK HIS BEST GIRL HOME, A FAR CRY FROM TODAY'S MODERN TECHNIQUES OF FRATERNIZING.
>
> MR. RALPH CHASE

The town center began to move away from the depot and Clark's store in the 1920s. The explosive growth of the automobile, the development of heavy trucks and of paved roads capable of bearing their weight signaled the decline of the railroad. The general store went first. Clark sold it and it went through a number of hands before my father bought it in 1924 – as it turned out, a bad business decision. He neglected to take insurance on the building and it burned to the ground the day after the sale became final. Rebuilding was not an option. He had paid cash and was completely wiped out. In any case, the focus of business activity was moving from the rail lines to an expanding highway system and the location as a commercial site was doomed. The service road behind Clark's store also disappeared. It had been called, prophetically, "Know Nothing Lane."

Rail service beyond Hyannis was discontinued after 1940. The rails themselves were torn up in 1967 and the bicycle path laid out a few years later. The center of town began to gravitate toward Town Hall. Over the years, the addition of the Fire Station, Police Facility, Eastham Superette and the renovation of Windmill Green have formed the nucleus of what could be an attractive, "walk-around" town center except for the fact that Route 6, four lanes wide and heavily traveled, bisects the entire area. Using twenty-twenty hindsight, it is sad that a means of having Route 6 by-pass the area were not devised earlier. Sixty years ago the depot closed and the trains stopped running – and we are still looking for a suitable town center.

CHAPTER 8

Oiling
the Roads

Eastham's roads in 1900 were all dirt and appropriate only for horse and buggy or horse-back travel. A summer visitor in his youth and, in retirement, one of Eastham's senior citizens, Freeman Hatch II, said of these roads,

> – we had only sand roads – a deep center rut for the horse and two side ruts for the wagon wheels. We used to figure from Eastham to Orleans put in a half a day. And Wellfleet – that was a whole day's trip and Chatham was almost out of the ques-tion. With a horse and wagon we would plan on staying overnight and come back the next day.

Hatch's comments come from an inter-view taped in 1963 by an Eastham historian, Colonel Clark, for the Historical Society and called, *Eastham Celebrities*. Hatch was a self-styled summer native who never, never spent a vacation away from Eastham and retired

*George Clark's store which housed
the Post Office and Library
as well as a general store.*

here after a distinguished engineering career. Clark's 1963 interview is the basis for much of the following.

Gasoline-powered cars were just beginning to appear in the U.S. in 1900. An estimated 8,000 cars were registered in the entire country that year. By 1908, the number had escalated 25 times to 200,000 automobiles. City roads had been paved, but very few of the roads in rural areas such as Cape Cod had been upgraded for automobile travel. Mr. Hatch, eighteen years old in 1908, described Eastham's approach to this problem as follows:

> The State's Public Works Commissioner thought that Eastham would be a good place to try out a system being used in Texas and California mixing oil with sand and rolling it out to make good roads. In a few weeks there arrived a car load of oil on the side track at the back of George Clark's store. We didn't know if it was crude petroleum just as pumped out of the ground, or residue remaining after the distillation of gasoline or kerosene. In any case, the first problem was to get it out of the tank car and onto the road.
>
> The stuff had the consistency of cold molasses and would not pour at normal temperatures. The bottom of the car was equipped with steam coils but the track was not elevated and we couldn't get at the outlets. Harvey Moore built a staging over the top of the car and an Edison, diaphragm-type, pump was mounted on top of this scaffold. A steam generator was attached to the

King's Highway prior to oiling.

coils and after a day and a half of forcing live steam through them, the oil was at pouring temperature.

Next we had to find a way to carry the oil to the road and spread it onto the sand. Somebody remembered the watering carts or street sprinklers used in cities such as Brockton or New Bedford. We brought one down, positioned it and started pumping. The hot oil flowed into the wagon and we were in business. Four horses were needed to yank the vehicle away from the siding and up to the section of the State road which had been prepared for the experiment. What trouble we had getting the tank truck up to the main road. Harnesses broke, the wagon barely held together.

The section to be oiled stretched from the present Hemenway Landing Road and Route 6 intersection, past the Town Hall and the Overlook Inn to the Methodist Church. About a mile of roadway had been prepared by spreading sand and leveling off the humps and valleys in the dirt road with a scraper. The sand road was ready to receive the oil.

No one had realized that the oil would cool off in the truck. The holes in the distributing pipe were now too

Oiling and leveling the road in front of Overlook Inn, 1908.
Horses driven by Dan Sparrow, author's father.

small. We had to go to larger diameter pipes with larger holes. With this revised system, the oil spewed out of the holes. But, the crew couldn't dilly-dally spreading the oil. Any delay and the oil cooled to the point that it refused to run. Once when this occurred, someone took the cap off the distributing pipe and rammed a red hot crow bar into the same. We found the crowbar some weeks later, 150 feet away over the side of the road.

After the oil had been set out on the roadway, it was covered with sand by hand and then a disc harrow drawn by a pair of horses blended the oil with the sand. After that, a horse drawn wooded roller leveled it out. And there was our road.

We soon learned that the oil provided us was far from ideal. It became very soft in the summer temperatures and as hard as a brick in winter time. When you drove a horse and wagon down that road, you had to carry a screwdriver with you and stop every so often when the

King's Highway after oiling, in front of Overlook Inn,
looking toward the present site of the Methodist Church.

horse became lame, to lift each hoof and clean out the oil and sand. Conversely, in winter time the horse would pick up those hard, brittle chunks of oil and the road was in rough shape.

The crude oil used in the first experiments was soon replaced with hot, liquid asphalt, a by-product of petroleum distillation. The term, oiled roads, is really a euphemism for asphalt/sand roads. For many years all of our paved roads were created, repaired or reconditioned in this fashion. At an early date the State switched to hot mix asphalt – higher viscosity asphalt mixed with sand and gravel, spreadable when hot but hard when cooled to ambient temperatures. Eastham began to use the hot mix on some of its roads after World War II. However, many of our roads to this day are repaired by "oiling" – sanding, spraying with hot asphalt and mixing the two.

CHAPTER 9

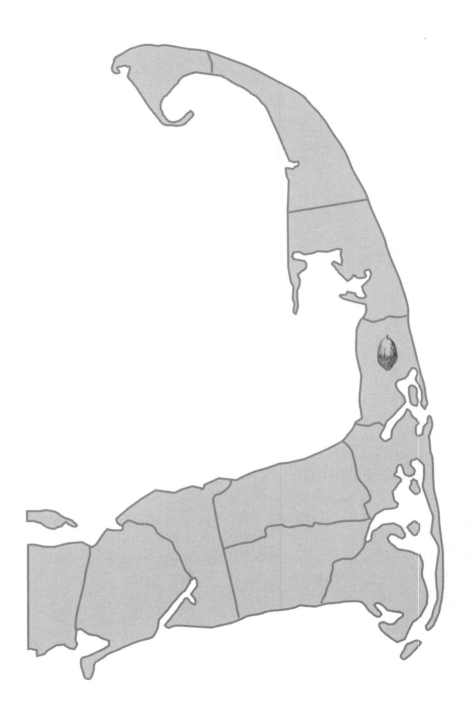

An Early Public Water Supply

Before the old King's Highway through Eastham was widened and straightened in 1935, it took a sharp left turn as it approached Salt Pond. Following the present Salt Pond Road, it rejoined what is now Route 6 at the traffic lights by the Seashore Visitor's Center. This section of the King's Highway was part of the road which was paved (or oiled) during the 1908 pioneering road work. I always enjoyed riding my bike from our home in Nauset to the Library because I could shop at Minnie Cole's candy store at the intersection of Salt Pond and Locust Roads, and then go across the street for a drink of water at the water trough with its hand-operated pump. In the picture Mrs. Cole's house and store were to the right and Salt Pond Road heads north toward the present set of lights on Route 6. Locust Road goes off to the left behind the pump. Mrs. Cole dealt mostly in penny candy such as licorice whips, candy coated peanuts called Boston Baked Beans or a sickly sweet, yellow, marshmallow confection that looked and tasted vaguely, like a banana. I needed the water to wash down the sugar.

Town Pump, before the road was oiled, Eastham's old Town Hall on the left side of the road.

The watering trough and pump had been installed after the Civil War and the site was a popular gathering spot for horses and buggies before they were displaced by the automobile. That it was an important part of the town activities was made clear in an essay entitled, *An Oration By the Town Pump*, written by my grandfather, Wilbur N. Sparrow in 1871. The pump compares itself, favorably, to most of the town officials as follows:

> *"The title of Town Treasurer – is rightly mine as guardian of the best treasure the town has. The Overseers of the Poor ought to make me their chairman, since I provide bountifully for the pauper, without expense to him who pays taxes. I am at the head of the Fire Department and am one of the physicians to the Board of Health. As a keeper of the peace all water drinkers will confess me equal to the Constable. I perform some of the duties of the Town Clerk by promulgating public notices when pasted on my front."*

The pump then goes on to boast about the superior qualities of its product...

"Here it is gentlemen, here is the good beverage!" "Walk up gentlemen, walk up!" Here is the unadulterated ale of father Adam better than cognac, Holland gin, Jamaica rum, strong beer or wine, of any price, and here it is by the hogshead or by the single glass and not a cent to pay. Walk up gentlemen and help yourselves."

Next comes a description of some of the customers who are sampling his wares. One is an honest, upright, hard-working laborer.

"You my friend will need another cupful to wash the dust out of your throat if it be as thick there as it is on your cowhide shoes. I see that you have trudged half a score of miles today; and like a wise man, have passed by the taverns and stopped only at the running brooks and well cribs. Otherwise betwixt fear without, and fire within, you would have been burnt to a cinder or melted down to nothing at all in the fashion of a jelly-fish."

Another customer is a serious drinker who has over-indulged...

"...make room for that other fellow who seeks my aid to quench the fiery fever of last night's potations which he drained from no cup of mine. Welcome most rubicund sir! You and I have been great strangers hitherto, nor to confess the truth, will my nose be anxious for a closer intimacy till the fumes of your breath be a little less potent. Mercy on you, man! The water absolutely hissed down your red hot gullet and is converted quite to

steam in the miniature fiery furnace...which you mistake for a stomach."

Children could also avail themselves of the free supply of aqua pura.

"Oh my little friends, you are let loose from school and come hither to scrub your blooming face, and drown the memory of certain schoolboy troubles in a draft from the town pump. Take it, pure as the current of your young life. Take it, and may your heart and tongue never be scorched with a fierier thirst than now."

One gentleman unwisely ignores the sales pitch.

"What! He limps past without so much as thanking me, as if my hospitable offers were meant only for people who have no wine cellars. Well, well sir – no harm done I hope. Go draw the cork and tip the decanter, but when your great toe shall set you a roaring it will be no affair of mine. If gentlemen love the titillation of the gout, it is all one to the town pump."

Finally, man's best friend can also avail himself of the pump's bounty.

"Thirsty dog with his red tongue lolling out, does not scorn my hospitality but stands on his hind legs and eagerly laps out of the trough. See how lightly he capers away again."

The document quoted here is signed Wilbur N. Sparrow, Eastham Mass 1871, but it does not record if, or when, the oration was delivered or by whom. My grandfather, seventeen at the time, was deaf and mute, a recent graduate of the Hartford Asylum for the Deaf and Dumb. The school was headed by Dr. Gallaudet, who went on to become President of Gallaudet College in Washington, D.C. The Hartford School's

English classes must have been out-standing.

After the main highway by-passed Salt Pond Road, the watering trough was moved to the Village Green. Fred Trahan installs the hand operated pump there every spring and passers-by can again quench their thirst at one of Eastham's pub-lic water supplies. Of course the sup-ply has to be tested frequently to be sure the water is not polluted. One test this past summer had an unac-ceptable level of contaminants and until the next test was negative, the town pump could no longer describe

Twenty-three-year-old Wilbur Norris Sparrow, taken in 1877, author of An Oration by the Town Pump.

its product as "...the unadulterated ale of father Adam...." It is still free but if the trend toward higher nitrate levels, and other contaminants, continues the town may be faced with the cost of a municipal water sup-ply and the town pump would have to delete its claim, " – by the hogshead or the single glass and not a cent to pay."

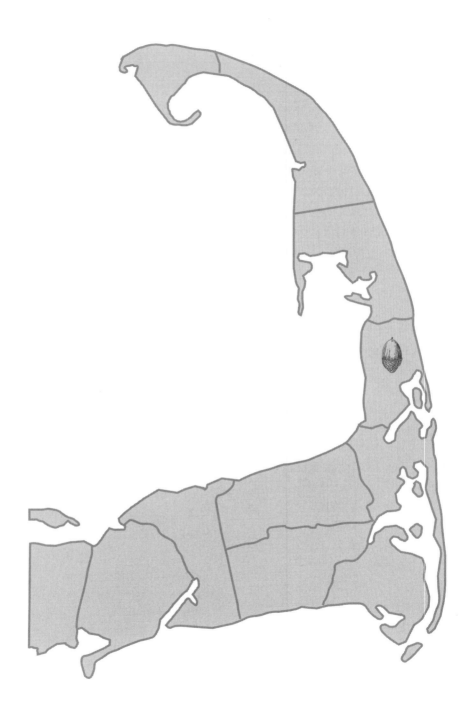

CHAPTER 10

Sam Brackett's Store[1]

Eastham had two social centers around the turn of the century, roughly the years from 1880 to 1930. These were Clark's store across the track from the Eastham depot (described in Chapter 7), and Brackett's store five miles to the north near the North Eastham depot. People came to these locations for the same reasons: to pick up their mail, passengers on the train, freight shipments, do their weekly shopping and get the latest gossip.

In the 1800s the Brackett family owned considerable farmland in North Eastham. Two brothers, Samuel and George, the last of twelve children by Elkanah and Achsah Brackett, began to diversify beyond farming. They built rental cottages on the West Shore near Campground Landing, and bought a general store in North Eastham from Arthur Cobb, probably a relative since their grandmother's name was Mercy Cobb. George pre-

---

[1] This story of Brackett's store is based on a number of sources – oral history interviews with Art Nickerson in 1982 and Art Benner in 1988, a letter to *The Cape Codder* written in 1950 by Benner's father, Art Senior, and printed in May 26, 2000 and Betty (Brackett) Latham's memories of her grandfather, Samuel F. Brackett, which she has been kind enough to share with me.

Sam Brackett's house across the street from his store on the right side of Massasoit Road, before the road had been oiled.

ferred to devote his energies to the family farm, which grew mainly asparagus and turnips, but his brother expanded the store and operated it as the Samuel F. Brackett General Store for over 60 years. The 1880s picture shows the store, on the right of what is now Massasoit Road and Sam Brackett's house across the street on the left.

Art Benner, Jr., whose family lived on Massasoit Road, just north of Brackett's store and were frequent customers, described the inside of the store:

> As you came in the entrance door, on your left was the big candy counter, which was the number one object. And then on the north wall were all the patent medicines. As you proceeded in, there was a counter with a big coffee grinder and a hand of bananas. If you went still further to go out to the back part, there were the buggy whips which hung in a little circular affair and also the sugar and flour barrels.
>
> On the south side of the store was a little cubicle where the bookkeeping was done. Also on the south side was another showcase with odds and ends and a big

Brackett's General Store.

counter with dry goods, yard goods. All shapes, sizes, colors and dimensions and so forth on rolls. Of course, people did more of their own millinery work in those days. And I remember there was a big iron safe where the bookkeeping was done. I suppose to keep their money and stuff.

Then there was a sort of separation, almost a partition between the two sides. Beyond the partition there was a big wooden box which had rubber boots, one of the necessities of the day. There were slickers, rain gear, all that sort of thing. A staircase led upstairs, just before you went out to the back part of the store. Up there they had dishwares and such things, odds and ends.

And if you went out to the next part of the building you'd be into where they did their deliveries, unloaded their eggs and the grain, and where George Wiley's delivery wagon was. There was a big, big ice chest out there where the soda pop and the salt pork and the

George Wiley standing beside his delivery wagon.

meat was kept. Downstairs from there was a molasses barrel where the molasses was kept. Someone left the spigot open one day and the barrel of molasses went all over the floor and we always smelled that nice aroma afterwards.

The next section out was where the grain and that sort of thing, coal, hardware and so forth, were kept. Beyond that was a sort of an enclosure for all the cartons and debris. Then there was a small, one car garage. Beyond that was the barn with its attached sheds. In the barn was a nice buggy, a rubber-tired buggy and an old Reo truck they had scrapped. The horse was kept off to one side of that. Another shed was just near the road from that.

Art Sr. added these details on the merchandise carried in the store:
There were more departments under his roof than in any store today. There were shoes, boots and dry goods, perfumes and toilet articles, drugs and stationery, to-

bacco and confectionery, jewelry, clocks, watches and Attleboro diamond rings.... The list goes on and on and concludes with...and then there were the miscellaneous items which included almost every item under the sun.

Whatever you needed Mr. Brackett had it in stock. It was simply a question of finding it. If you wanted a bottle of tonic it was buried deep under the corn beef and for lack of space some of hardware was kept in with the salt pork.

Art Jr. grew nostalgic as he remembered some of the store's departments:

The penny candy was a little bit larger than the nickel bars are today. It would take thirty cents now to buy a pennies worth of candy then. When you paid your grocery bill – which most people did semiannually or whatever, when the crops or shellfish came in – Mr. Brackett would always fill up a big bag of candy. That's all I was interested in, the candy, never mind the rest of it, you know. I'll always remember that. The candy, the penny candies were chocolate and licorice and hard balls, nougatines, old-fashioneds, bolsters and some sort of coconut thing. They were so nicely done, you know. The quality was there. I always think of that – gee, if you had a case of that you could retire today.

And then there were the patent medicines. You could get Lydia Pinkhams, Father Johns, Musterole – the worst thing that ever happened. The cure was worse than the disease. Fletchers Castoria was another one, that was an old standby. And the worst thing, I think – the very worst of the worst was castor oil. That was horrid, terrible stuff.

Art Nickerson, who lived only a few hundred yards from the store, has these memories of the general store.

> They held everything in there. You could go up and get yourself men's shoes, men's pants, shirts, a pair of bloomers, stockings, dresses, jug of molasses (you brought your own jug), kerosene, groceries and meats, salt pork. Then they had hay, grain and fertilizer. Fertilizer would be on the honor system. It would come by freight car over by Roach's plant where the depot was. If you ordered two tons from Samuel F. Brackett & Son you would go over and get forty, 100 pound bags yourself, you didn't ask anyone. When I was twelve years old I ordered a ton myself from Brackett and got trusted for it. Twelve years old.

Art Benner, Sr., also commented on Brackett's generosity in financial matters.

> The matter of shopping was extremely simple. You just ordered everything you needed from Mr. Brackett's general store. We didn't even have to say "charge it." He knew that. Liberal long time credit was extended and the more you owed the better customer you were. It was when you owed several hundred dollars that you got the best service. If you needed $500 or $1,000, it wasn't necessary to go to the bank. Mr. Brackett would oblige.

Samuel F. was a typical Cape Codder of his time. In addition to running the general store he grew asparagus and turnips on farmland where the Eastham Catholic Church is now located and also maintained about 15 rental cottages near Campground Landing. Betty Latham remembers having to help clean these cottages when in her teens. She also remembers him spending long hours in his office struggling with the accounts of all three of his ventures.

Brackett's store prospered for many years and the owner was greatly admired for his kindness and generosity as well as his business acumen. His son, Samuel H. Brackett, came into the store in the '20s and the company name changed to Samuel F. Brackett & Son. But then at the start of the 1930s two events brought serious problems. During the Depression most of their customers had severe cash flow problems. Then two supermarkets, A & P and First National, opened stores in Orleans. Also, Samuel F., born in 1864, was getting along in years. The combined efforts of father and son were to no avail. The store shut its doors forever in the middle 1930s.

Art Benner, Jr., remembered its last days.

> He had a going-out-of-business sale. There were high-buttoned shoes and all sorts of objects you hadn't seen for quite a while. They held auctions and I was there one evening when that was going on. It was interesting to see such a variety of things, spices and little cans of this and little cans of that. But that was the beginning of the end. That's when it wound up.

The basic reason for the demise of both Brackett's and Clark's stores was probably the same – automobiles and trucks replaced the trains and new roads built to handle the increased traffic bypassed them. The Brackett building was sold after World War II to a mitten manufacturer who took down the barn and a number of the attached sheds. Then the Delaney family bought the remaining building and now lease a portion of it to Eastham's Council on Aging who use it for their Thrift Shop. All traces of the across-the-street Millennium Grove have disappeared but the front of Brackett's store building has changed very little and old timers like me feel a nostalgic twinge as we leave off our Thrift Shop contributions.

Today, shopping at the superstores such as Orleans' Stop & Shop and Shaws or the Hyannis Mall certainly doesn't have the charm or friendliness of the old general stores. But, residents and tourists who patronize many of the Outer Cape's small, general stores are received with a warmth approaching that of the long gone Sam Brackett or George Clark markets. I stop into Eastham's Superette at least once a day and am comforted by the relaxed (except in July and August), first-name-basis reception. However, I do miss the penny candy case with its display of irresistible delights such as licorice whips, Boston Baked Bean candy-coated peanuts or yellow, marshmallow bananas.

CHAPTER 11

The Quahog Wars

Many of the items stocked by Brackett's store – slickers, rubber boots, fishing tackle, hay, grain, fertilizer – reflect the fact that most of its customers earned a living by farming, fishing or shellfishing and frequently all three. Freedom to take shellfish in waters of Cape Cod Bay, with its abundant beds of scallops, clams and quahogs, had been a zealously guarded privilege since Colonial days.

Quahogs or hard shell clams were especially important to Eastham's residents. The shellfish made up a substantial portion of the diet of many of us. Quahog chowder was made with meats chopped in a wooden bowl, fried pork scraps, milk, potatoes, onions and a big chunk of butter – no thickener and absolutely no tomatoes. Quahog pie was made with the same ingredients except less milk and all encased in a flaky crust. Leftover quahogs could be incorporated into fritters for Sunday breakfast, served with plenty of ketchup.

Town reports listed the quahog permits issued and just about everyone capable of wielding a bullrake or scratcher held a permit. In 1915, for example, the town issued 75 per-

Quahoging from a catboat with a bullrake.

mits, 49 for the flats and 32 for the Bay. This was before quahog draggers were used. Quahogers went out in catboats in the Bay, pulled a heavy
bullrake with a wooden handle along the bottom, hauled up the loaded
rake and sorted out the good mollusks from the rocks, shells, seaweed
and general muck. It was brutally hard work and required being in top
physical condition.

In the early 1900s the Town of Eastham and Wellfleet engaged in
the "Quahog Wars" – a series of heated exchanges of speeches and published broadside charges and countercharges that reached as far as the
Massachusetts Supreme Court and the Statehouse. The issue was a
town's authority to control the taking of quahogs from its bay waters.

The acting chairman of the Eastham Board of Selectmen on March
28, 1911 wrote to the Supreme Court as follows:

> For 150 years from 1764, when Massachusetts was a
> province up to the present day, 1911, both the Provin-
> cial Government and the State of Massachusetts have
> recognized in their laws the right of a town to control
> and preserve the shellfish within its own limit.

He was protesting Senate Bill No. 277, sponsored by the Town of
Wellfleet, which gave citizens of both towns unlimited rights to shell-

fishing in the neighboring town. Wellfleet's town officials claimed that under a 1904 agreement, the residents of both towns should have such unlimited rights. Eastham officials protested that the written document describing the 1904 Act contained the phrase, "the selectmen of its town may grant," and that the Eastham voters would not have accepted it otherwise.

The acrimonious dispute between the two towns arose early in the 1900s when the Wellfleet shellfish beds had been depleted because of the large number of quahogers in the town. A large fleet of Wellfleet fishing vessels came into Eastham waters and, according to an Eastham Town Selectman,

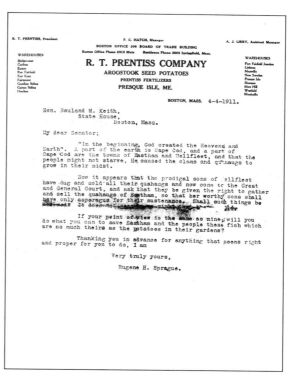

Letter from Eugene Sprague

"early and late took enormous quantities of quahogs." They continued to defy the Eastham selectmen's orders to cease and a complaint was issued against one of them. The quahoger appealed the lower court's guilty verdict to the Massachusetts Supreme Court and, after a full jury trial, was again found guilty and fined.

His counsel appealed this verdict on exceptions. The town of Wellfleet, not waiting for a decision from the latest legal maneuver, brought Bill No. 277 to the Senate. Outraged Eastham residents flooded their Senator with mail. The letter from Eugene Sprague to Senator

Rouland M. Keith conveys a skeptical attitude toward the perfidious Wellfleet citizens that is typical of the conflict.

The heart of the matter came down to a 1904 Senate bill (No. 264) that took all powers of regulating quahogs from Eastham's Town Meeting and gave it to Eastham's selectmen. The Bill contained the wording: "The Selectmen <u>may</u> grant quahoging licenses to residents of Wellfleet and Orleans. The Wellfleet Selectmen claimed that, in a joint meeting, the boards of both towns had agreed verbally to the wording, "<u>shall</u> grant," although no written record of this agreement existed. Attorney Heman Harding from Chatham rendered an opinion for the Eastham Selectmen, classic in its simplicity, that stated, "I am satisfied that the word 'may' means may and not shall." Doubts as to whether the Eastham Town Meeting had ever accepted the provisions of the 1904 Bill 264 further complicated the situation.

In 1911 when Senate Bill 277 came to the floor for action, the Town of Eastham spent substantial sums of money for lawyers' fees and for town officials' travel expenses to Boston to testify in the "quahog matter" as the 1911 Town Report put it. The Bill failed to pass and Eastham's 1912 Town Meeting passed an article that unequivocally accepted the provisions of the 1904 Bill. Wellfleet's fishermen had to cease their activities in Eastham waters.

Now, 90 years later, Eastham residents may regret their success. Oysters shun the Eastham waters, preferring to reproduce in the more favorable areas north of our border. Why they are more favorable is a mystery to everyone including Eastham's Natural Resources Officer, Henry Lind. His staff has researched the subject exhaustively and has yet to identify the reason. One of his junior constables advanced the theory that oysters flourish in the dirtier Wellfleet water; evidence perhaps that the Eastham-Wellfleet quahog issue is still alive nearly a century after the initial conflict. In 1999, Wellfleet raised the cost of its yearly out-of-towner quahoging permit from $25.00 to $130.00.

CHAPTER 12

Bullrake Quahoging[1]

Never assume anything. Teachers emphasized this point in my basic science courses, but I ignored their words of wisdom while writing the previous chapter. Attending a Christmas cocktail party shortly after it appeared in *The Cape Codder*, I talked with Eastham's authority on our history, Art Nickerson, and he nailed me. I asked if he had read the Quahog Wars piece and did he like it. He answered,

> "Yes I have. No I didn't. Have you ever used a bullrake?"
>
> "No I haven't, why?"
>
> "You forgot that the tide goes up and down and you have to carry three or four bullrake handles of different lengths."

I had guessed that a 20-foot pole might be adequate under all conditions and so had equipped my bullrake quahoger with one pole of that length.

---

[1] Much of this is based on Warren Darling's Quahoging Out of Rock Harbor, 1890 - 1930. The rights are held by Warren Darling's three children. The book has been reprinted and is on sale. It's a classic.

How to get more information on this point? I knew no one who had used a bullrake but then I recalled that about 17 years ago a former Orleans resident, Mr. Warren S. Darling, had written a booklet on the subject – *Quahoging Out of Rock Harbor 1890 - 1930*. As a teenager Mr.

Eben Cummings with bullrake.

Darling had gone bullrake shellfishing with his father, Nathan C. Darling. Digging the document out of my files, I found that Art was right. The bullrake quahoger typically carried three poles, for example: 28, 42 and 56 feet long.

The beautifully written discourse on bullrake quahoging explained, for me, the term "bullrake." These three-feet-wide, rectangular iron rakes had four semi-circular hoops and were fitted with as many as 25 four-inch, dagger-shaped teeth positioned along the front lip. They weighed at least 20 pounds and more than double that when hauled up from the bottom of the bay. The strength of a bull was needed to use them. The picture of Eben Cummings, taken in the early 1900s by his brother H. K. Cummings, show the bullrake in some detail.

Mr. Darling tells of the hardy shellfishermen who went out of Rock Harbor in a catboat driven by a sail of a 1^1/$_2$ h.p., one-lung, gas engine. I began to wonder how anyone could handle a 56-foot pole with forty or more pounds of rake loaded with quahogs on one end while standing on a pitching, rocking, 28-foot boat. Mr. Darling supplied the answers in his detailed essay on the Bullrake.

This method of quahoging was used for relatively few years, from the turn of the century to about 1930. Fishermen worked from a broad-beamed catboat, about 28 feet in length and almost as wide, positioned in Cape Cod Bay between Wellfleet and Brewster. The boat was anchored fore and aft in 10 to 40 feet of water depending on the tide and location. Favored places were the Channel where the Target Ship SS *James Longstreet* was eventually grounded on the "back-of-the-flats" – the area just beyond the point you could reach by foot at low tide on the Orleans, Eastham and Wellfleet flats of Cape Cod Bay.

Quahoging in forty feet of water obviously required the longest, 56-foot, pole. This was made of two or more sections of straight-grained, southern hard pine, securely joined together, slightly tapered and with a crossbar or tee on the larger end and the rake at the other. Mr. Darling writes,

> One of the most beautiful sights I can imagine is that of a quahog boat – with the quahoger pulling up his rake – the graceful, smooth curve of his homemade, 56-foot pole arching across the boat just before the tee touched the water twenty, or more, feet away. Great care had to be taken in matching the natural direction of the bend of each piece to achieve the smooth arch of a well proportioned pole. Walt Disney might have filmed its rhythmic undulations and set them to music.

> "THE GRACEFUL, SMOOTH CURVE OF HIS HOMEMADE, 56-FOOT POLE ARCHING ACROSS THE BOAT JUST BEFORE THE TEE TOUCHED THE WATER TWENTY, OR MORE, FEET AWAY. WALT DISNEY MIGHT HAVE FILMED ITS RHYTHMIC UNDULATIONS AND SET THEM TO MUSIC."
>
> MR. WARREN S. DARLING

Darling's father made his own poles. The first step was selecting the pine stock from Nickerson Lumber (now Mid Cape Lumber). Two important qualities were a clear grain extending the length of the 28 foot long, two by two inch square stock and the amount and direction of the greatest bend. The selected pine pieces were planed and sanded to form round, slightly tapered sections and then, with the grain running horizontal to the ground, spliced to make poles of varying lengths.

Eben bringing in a load of quahogs and "shack."

Finally, a short, eight to ten inch piece fitted to the larger end of the tapered pole formed the tee-shaped handle.

The rakes were not available off the shelf but rather, made to the quahoger's individual specification by the local blacksmith. The net attached to the iron frame work was at first woven by the quahoger or his wife until a heavy tennis net with $1^1/_2$" mesh was available from A. F. Smith and Sons. "The net made a bag two and a half to three feet deep" when loaded with quahogs and "shack," their name for all the non-quahog bottom material found in the net.

> The rake was attached to the pole by overlapping the rake's tapered tail, or tine, with the small end of the tapered pole and driving an oval, egg-shaped ring down onto the overlapped tine and pole. They were one unit now, but the pole could be changed quickly by driving the oval ring in the reverse direction. At the end of the day the rake and tee end were removed and the poles laid on deck with the ends dragging in the water on the way back to port.

When the catboat reached the selected position in the bay, the fisherman headed into the tide, set an anchor, snubbed it on a stern cleat and continued to run into the tide until about 600 feet of line had paid out. At this point he killed the engine, snubbed the line, and when the forward momentum had pulled the line taut, he threw out the bow anchor as far as possible. The anchor line was known as the "warp" or the "rode." If all had been done properly, he was now firmly anchored, fore and aft, heading into the tide.

After assembling the rake, pole and tee he was ready to go to work, to dig up quahogs from "an area of the sea bottom roughly the length of the boat and as wide as possible without missing any strips or raking the same area twice." The first few passes were made by "running the rode," that is, putting the rake, teeth up, on the rode and sliding it down the line "with a rapid, hand-over-hand motion. When the tee came to hand it was used to twist the pole and flip the rake off the rode." Now came the really back-breaking work. With the rake's teeth set into the sea bottom he moved them "through the top layer by a continuing rhythmic series of short, hard, backward-downward jerks of the tee end of the pole."

While doing this he was also "inching backwards at the very edge of the boat" until he reached the stern. The catboat picture in the previous chapter shows the narrow gunnel where the fisherman crept along while pulling the rake through the bottom on the bay. In this stage the bend in the pole was critical. The tide pressing on the submerged, arched pole held the rake into the bottom so that it "fished" properly. Finally, after reaching the stern, he walked forward until the pole was vertical, hauled the net full of quahogs and "shack" up and dumped it on the culling board. Now his son had the task of sorting out the net's contents, throwing overboard the "stones, old shells, snails and seaweed" and saving the few quahogs while the quahoger repeated the operation. He ran the rode for several more passes and then threw the rake out to the left and right of the rode so as to cover new territory.

Inching along the edge of the boat, bow to stern, called for the balancing skill of a high-wire circus performer. The tee at the end of the pole was his only support. This was unconnected to the boat and moved up when the boat moved down. With a gentle breeze and small waves to add to the swell it might be rather pleasant, but just imagine a strong cross wind with the boat pitching and rolling on a heavy swell. The quahoger had to pull the rake through the surface layer of the bay's bottom while at the same time edging backward and bending and dodging to "compensate for the motion of the boat."

These men must have been in top-notch physical condition to do the hard, grinding work day after day. Mr. Darling mentions some of them – his father, Nathan, and his partner, Reed Walker, Cap'n Benny Nickerson, Eben Cummings, Herman Tayler, Abner Snow and John Ryder. His book gives a complete description of every phase of bullrake fishing – much more on pole construction, different techniques to handle varying tides, water and weather conditions, various kinds of quahogs, details about the catboat and its one-lung engine, the economics of the quahog trade in those days, encounters with whales and swordfish, the fun he had as a boy helping his father work the bay with a bullrake, and much more. I highly recommend it.

CHAPTER 13

Weir Fishing

Shellfishermen taking quahogs on the West Shore had to compete with the weir fishermen for digging room on the flats. From the late 1800s to the 1930s weir or trap fishing flourished in Eastham. Fish weirs took up all the available space on the six miles of its coastline along Cape Cod Bay. These were the so-called low water weirs suitable to the bay's six-to-nine foot tides with a gently sloping coast covered with water at high tide and barely wet at low tide. The more common deep-water weirs were used in areas where the bottom is always covered with water even at low tide.

Joseph C. Lincoln in his book, *Cape Cod Yesterday*, gives a description of weirs,

> – deep-water and low-water weirs have a long leader, a fence constructed of poles driven into the sand at equal distances apart, the spaces between closed with nets and hung on ropes. The upper edges are buoyed with wooden floats and the lower edges are weighed with lead.

Setting out poles for weir fishing.

In the case of the low-water weir, the leader extends from the high tide water near the shore to a point where the water is shallow or the bottom is bare at low tide. Fish surrounding the net at high tide are forced to swim along it until they reach a trap at the low water point, a parallel net forming a narrow passage leading to a circular enclosure with a small opening at the end of the leader. Most of the fish mill about in the trap, not bright enough to escape via the small opening. The owner rides out in a cart at low tide, pitches his catch into that cart and rides home.

The next stop for wagons coming off the flats was the icehouse where the fish were iced down, packed in barrels and brought to the depot for shipment to the Boston and New York markets. As many as two rail cars were filled and sent to market on a good day. If the tide was such that the fish could not be brought in and packed in time for the scheduled departure, the train waited for the catch to be ready for shipment.

Bringing in fish from weir net with horse and wagon.

In another of Col. Clark's interviews with Eastham celebrities, a local fisherman described the kinds of fish caught in the weirs. John Forrester Crosby came down from Nova Scotia at the turn of the century to work on the weirs. According to Forrester, (everyone used his middle name), in early spring the main catch was herring, which was shipped to markets in Boston and New York and used primarily for bait. These and the succeeding fish were packed in ice, sometimes in boxes, but mostly in barrels. Next came mackerel, "in great abundance," followed in July and August by bluefish.

Weakfish, also called "squeateague," were next. They were large fish, so large that when packed with heads resting on the bottom of the barrel, their tails stuck out over the top. The name, "weakfish" comes from their very soft jaws, which sometime tear away when hooked, so that the fisherman is left with just a jaw bone on the line. They have disappeared from Cape Cod waters.

Flounder were also plentiful in the weir nets, and in the fall, tuna appeared. The latter were so large that one sometimes filled a wagon cart. Tuna were not highly regarded as a food fish in those days as evidenced by their nickname, "horse mackerel." A 500-pound horse mackerel had to be clubbed or hacked to death before going into the cart, without damaging the trap enclosure. Lincoln says,

> The amount of damage a five-hundred pound fish can
> do to a weir is considerably more than a little. When at
> last he is killed and rolled inboard, the tuna is good for
> nothing. Bring him ashore, throw him out on the beach
> and let him rot in the sun. One of our most fragrant
> memories is of a dead horse mackerel lying on the shore
> to windward of the weir shanties at Quivet Neck.

Of course, the various kinds of fish did not appear and disappear in neat, orderly fashion from spring to fall. At low tide, the trap generally held a mixture, called "culch," of a variety of marketable as well as trash fish. An occasional cod, haddock, plaice or tautog (blackish) might be found on a lucky day, along with some of the species described above, as well as the less desirable sculpin, skate, blowfish, crabs and squid.

Horse mackerel and some of the less desirable species of trash fish are now regarded as prize catches. Tuna salad sandwich is a standard lunch counter or lunch box item and the Japanese pay premium prices for tuna air freighted to Tokyo to become sushi. Squid becomes calamari in many Italian restaurants and skate, as raie, is served in gourmet American restaurants and has long been a delicacy in French bistros.

The low-water weirs have not been used on the West Shore flats for some time. My earliest memories date back to the late 1920s and I never saw the nets and poles there. I feel deprived after reading Joseph Lincoln's reminiscences:

> As a boy I never refused an invitation to ride out to a fish
> weir with its owner. Always we rode in a blue truck-
> wagon, behind a plodding horse or a yoke of oxen. You
> started out when the tide was ebbing and if, homeward
> bound, you forded the inshore channel before the

water was up to the wheel hubs, that was all that was necessary.

On a summer afternoon, perched on the boxed seat of a smelly truck-wagon, with old Beriah Hallett beside you, his whiskered jaws moving as he chewed his tobacco, and the feet of the oxen (plop-plopping) or (splash-splashing) as they moved across the flats or waded the channels – that was good enough fun for a couple of bare-footed, freckle-faced youngsters.

Weir fishing may have been fun for the youngsters but it was brutally hard work for the fishermen. It is still practiced in some New England areas but no longer on the Outer Cape Cod Bay tidal flats. The supply of fish is greatly diminished and there are easier ways to make a living. A representative of Eastham's Natural Resources Department tells me that they can issue permits for weir fishing nets but none have been issued for years. In addition, the permitting process might be difficult in view of the importance of recreational activities on the waters of West Shore – swimming, quahoging, charter boat fishing, or just strolling the two miles or so of flats at low tide, especially when Mother Nature cooperates by providing a glorious First Encounter Beach sunset.

Twentieth Century

Against a backdrop of two World Wars, Eastham and its citizens survived the Depression, Prohibition and the coming of the Cape Cod National Seashore. The sea continued to be vitally important as young men captained ocean-going vessels, rumrunners cruised the Cape waters while their jettisoned cargoes contributed to Eastham teenager's pocket money, and Eastham's ponds, ocean and bay beaches attracted large numbers of summer visitors and retired people.

Asparagus and turnip farming enjoyed a bright heyday until tourism and retirees made the land too valuable for farming. An eighteen hole, private golf course, played by such notables as Bobby Jones and Francis Ouimet, helped to ease the economic pressures of the Depression.

This section also describes how young Eastham residents relaxed with spare time pursuits such as pre-TV radio, movies, baseball and shooting rats at the dump, how their mothers adapted to the changing styles in shopping, how Cape citizens reacted when the Federal Government established the Seashore in their area and why the author, his uncle and his brother, along with many other Eastham ex-patriots, returned to their home town.

CHAPTER 14

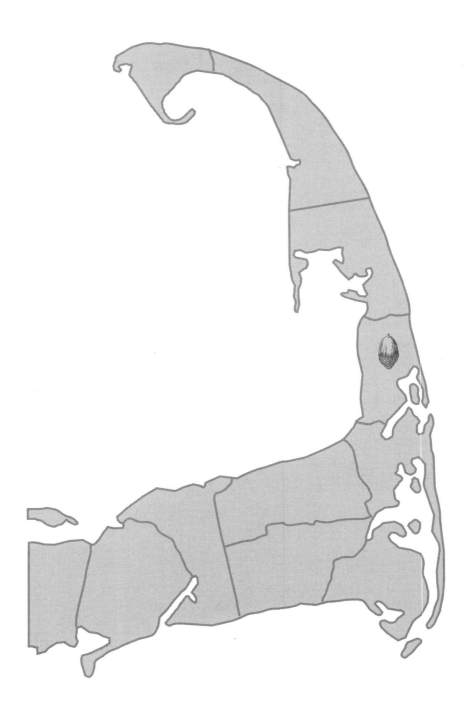

The Town
Dump

One of today's pressing problems, waste disposal, wasn't even mentioned in the 1900 Town Report. In 1926 the town spent fifty dollars to acquire an acre of land for the town dump, the first record of any expenditure of that sort. Up to then town employees included a Weigher of Coal, a Pound Keeper, Viewers of Fences and Field drivers but no Dump Attendant. In 1942 Charles Escobar was appointed to the post of Dump Custodian, the town's first such worker. (More about Charlie later.)

Getting rid of the waste generated by an Eastham's year 2000 population of 5,000 people (20,000 in the summer time), is an expensive proposition. Eastham's budget for operation of the Transfer Station and Recycling Center plus transport and incineration of the solid waste amounted to about $380,000 in year 2000 and the town spent $1.2 million to put a waterproof cap over the area where the collected waste had been buried under a layer of sand for many years.

Before World War II when the Town's annual budget for waste disposal was close to zero, we went to the "dump," a sand pit dug in an uninhabited, pitch pine forest and probably the one acre purchased in 1926, once every few months to discard a few pieces of rubbish. The family dog gobbled down the table scraps and other garbage went to the pigs or the chickens. Organic waste unsuitable for animals was thrown into a pit dug in the backyard and covered with sand when full.

There wasn't much non-garbage rubbish either because we were into recycling in a big way. Thrifty Yankees – survivors of Cape Cod's hard times that culminated in the 1930s Depression – threw very little into that sand pit dump. Fruits and vegetables, jams and jellies were preserved at home in recycled glass containers. Plastics were materials of the future. Every family had its paper/string/rag saver and large barns and out buildings were great for storage of bits of metal, lumber and non-functioning farm equipment or household appliances that "needed work." Tired household furnishings and appliances helped newlyweds to set up housekeeping or graced the dwellings of less fortunate friends.

As youngsters my friends and I spent a lot of time at the sand pit dump. We went there with our air guns and later 22-caliber rifles, for target practice on tin cans and bottles or to shoot at the rats that infested the place. At the same location as now, off Old Orchard Road, it was just an isolated deep pit in the sandy soil at the end of a dirt lane, one half mile away from the main road (now Route 6). We didn't worry about wounding anyone, there was no attendant and very few dump users. Another, and perhaps more persuasive, reason for visiting the dump was the urge to rummage through the dump's contents. The imagined treasures rarely materialized, the prizes we brought home mother usually made us take back, post haste.

Supervision of the dump area came under the Highway Surveyor, an elected official in those days, and Mr. N. A. Nickerson, Sr., served in this position for many years starting in 1927. After he retired in 1964 the Board of Selectmen acted as the Highway Surveyor for a few years and then in 1970 the Department of Public Works assumed responsibility for the waste disposal area.

The Town had to operate a more formalized waste disposal site after World War II as Eastham's winter and summer populations skyrocketed along with the amounts of waste per capita. Our waste handling facility evolved through succeeding stages – sand pit to Sanitary Landfill to Transfer Station to combined Transfer, Recycling Center and now a Swap Shop has been added to the complex. At first, each stage meant more equipment and more personnel and more land. Perhaps the most colorful stage came when the accumulated waste could no longer be left to decay in the summer sun. To keep animals out of debris, and the odor down, the Town added a tractor and a waste disposal attendant to cover the accumulated waste daily with a layer of sand and the dump became the Sanitary Landfill.

Charlie Ecobar, Dump Custodian and King of the Skunkers in his youth.

Charlie Escobar's position as the first Dump Custodian must have been a part-time, one or two days a week, job because the annual dump budget was only $250. This was the same Charlie Escobar, Eastham's "King of the Skunkers," whose exploits in capturing the smelly animals I described in my book, *Growing Up On Cape Cod*. His father, Tony, took the position when Charlie was drafted into the Army the next year. Tony was one of a succession of Dump Custodians who served until the Public Works Department assumed responsibility for the Sanitary Land-fill operations in 1970.

The dump area grew along with the population. Paving of Old Orchard Road provided ready access and the area expanded to its present 45 acres. Going to the dump on weekends became a social event, vacationers renewing acquaintances with the natives, forming new friendships and discussing Town political vagaries. At election time aspirants to a seat on the Board of Selectmen had to put in an appearance on Saturday morning and chat up the voters. I served my dump time when running for Selectman in 1991. The day after election (I won), a friend called to say he had just returned from the dump and found several little old ladies asking for that nice young man who helped them with their bags of garbage.

> GOING TO THE DUMP ON WEEKENDS BECAME A SOCIAL EVENT, VACATIONERS RENEWING ACQUAINTANCES WITH THE NATIVES, FORMING NEW FRIENDSHIPS AND DISCUSSING TOWN POLITICAL VAGARIES.

Empty glass bottles occupy a lot of space and so the Landfill managers encouraged users to break the discarded glass containers in order to reduce the volume of the waste. Early on, the glass disposal area featured a wood fence and, (10 feet beyond), a cement wall – an irresistible target for hurled bottles and jars. Once I was happily disposing of our weekly glass collection in this manner when a young attendant commented, "You know, psychiatrists charge $25 or this therapy." (This was 20 years ago.)

The Town hired N. A. Nickerson and Sons, operated by descendants of Mr. Nickerson, Sr., to bury the daily accumulation of debris. Charlie Escobar resumed his work at the dump as an N. A. Nickerson employee and became something of a legend at the facility. He was conscientious, reliable and a helpful worker, as I learned on one hot, August Saturday.

I had, inadvertently, discarded a black plastic garbage bag which we were using to transport several of my mother's hooked rugs. Learning of my mistake a few hours later, I rushed to the dump and enlisted Charlie's aid in retrieving the valuable and treasured rugs. He hopped on his front-end loader and maneuvered it to sort through the 15-foot high piles of garbage bags waiting for transfer and burial in the landfill area. An hour passed as he methodically went through each pile, breaking open bags to reveal their contents. Every pile had been examined, no rugs had been sighted and I was ready to quit but he insisted on a second inspection. Under this blazing August afternoon sun the garbage exuded an almost visible cloud of lobster and shellfish smells along with other, equally powerful, aromas. But, he persisted and, miraculously, we spotted the rugs. They were largely undamaged and I was able to avoid a marital crisis.

With this kind of devoted service, we and most other Eastham citizens, were willing to tolerate his practice of screening the incoming waste and sequestering anything he considered to be of value. The grounds around his home on Old Schoolhouse Road assumed the aspect of a slightly upscale adjunct to the Town waste disposal area – to the considerable annoyance of neighbors.

In the late 1980s the town fathers were forced to rethink the landfill concept. The waste, piled up and covered with sand, grew to a sizeable hill on the landfill site. At one point the town's modest waste disposal fee structure encouraged neighboring town citizens to bring their refuse to Eastham. The hill grew enormously and the imposing mound was dubbed Mount Zannoni after the then current Chairman of the Board of Selectmen.

Over the years there had been little control over the kinds of waste put into the landfill and tests on neighboring wells showed signs of contamination suspected to come from hazardous materials leached out of the accumulated waste by rainfall. The immediate solution was to close the landfill and send the waste off Cape. The dump went through another name change, Transfer Station. Compacted waste went into a trailer and then to a Rochester, Massachusetts incinerator. The daily mound of odoriferous garbage became a thing of the past and dump picking was much less productive. The services of N. A. Nickerson's firm and Charlie, were no longer needed and Charlie's home waste storage collection ceased to grow.

Capping the landfill with a water-impervious top was a longer term solution to the suspected pollution from the landfill leachate and in fact our state mandated this action. Now, 1.2 million dollars later, Mount Zannoni is an attractive grass covered, capped hill, tests on the water from adjacent wells show little or no hazardous materials, and the area required for waste handling has shrunk considerably.

Shipping waste 100+ miles and paying to have it burned costs a lot more than simply covering it with sand and so the current emphasis is on recycling to reduce the amount of transported waste. The list of materials isolated at the Transfer Station and shipped away for reuse keeps growing – newspapers, magazines, cardboard, glass bottles, tin cans, plastic bottles, metals, motor oil – encouraged and facilitated by our active and admirable Recycling Committee. Another of their programs directed at the use of home composter units, helps to reduce the need to handle garbage and other organic waste at the Transfer Station. The most recent addition to our recycling efforts is a swap shop. Housed in a building on the site and dubbed "The Stock Market," it accepts and stores usable items, free for the taking by any Transfer Station visitor.

Now, I have a strong sense of déjà vu. We are coming full circle, getting close to the 75-year-ago condition of almost a total recycle. More and more of our waste is being productively utilized – recycled, burned for energy, composted for soil betterment or put to good use by second owners. Land requirements are shrinking; the extensive landfill area has been transformed into grass-covered Mount Zannoni. Our Transfer/Recycle/Swap Shop facility is a more business-like, impersonal place than the old sand pit or the landfill but it is also a cleaner, more scenic-aroma-environmentally friendly spot.

CHAPTER 15

Harvesting Prohibition's Flotsam and Jetsam

On Sundays in summer the shores of Eastham's Salt Pond are crowded with vacationing visitors armed with rakes, hoes, shovels and other digging implements. The crowd is after quahogs that have been grown from seed, planted in Salt Pond by our Natural Resources Department and made available to the public only on Sunday. It is one of our most popular tourist attractions and few of the amateur, sometimes neophyte, shellfishermen go home empty handed.

Driving past Salt Pond on a Sunday morning, I am reminded of similar scenes on the flats and inlets of the West Shore, 70 or more years ago. In those days the objective was not quahogs but bottles of liquor abandoned by rumrunners who were being pursued by the law. Rumrunning was an occupation created by the short-lived 18th Amendment to the United States Constitution, enacted in 1921 and repealed in 1933, which prohibited the production, importing, sale, transport and export of alcoholic beverages.

For most Americans over the age of 65 the word "Prohibition" (the commonly used

Typical rumrunning boat.

term for the 18th Amendment), evokes images of Federal Agents breaking open kegs of beer with axes and dumping the contents into the
sewer, or Chicago-based gangster, Al Capone, wearing a white, snap-
brim felt hat and scowling into the camera as he protests his lack of
knowledge of the perpetrators of the Valentine's Day murders. Although
President Herbert Hoover called it a "Noble Experiment," the 18th
Amendment is now generally regarded as the most ineffective, damaging and even stupidest United Sates law ever adopted. It did little or
nothing to stop the use of these beverages, led to the proliferation of
bootlegging hoodlums such as Capone and a host of other gangsters and
encouraged disregard for the country's laws.

Despite the disastrous effect on much of the country, Prohibition
had less impact on, and may have even benefitted, residents of sparsely
populated coastal areas with isolated beaches, such as Cape Cod. Much
of the illegal hard liquor used during Prohibition came from off-shore
sources and the contraband goods could be landed on the Cape's sandy,
shelving beaches with ease and no great fear of detection. The latter
years of Prohibition overlapped the early part of the Depression and the
money generated by the rumrunners was most welcome.

Reliable data on the amounts of money generated by rumrunning are
hard to find. A hint comes from information provided me a few years ago
by a former Eastham rumrunner and a neighbor of ours, Bud Cummings.

His data suggests that one crew operating a boat between the Cape and foreign supply ships stationed beyond the 12-mile limit (known as Rum Row), might have realized $200,000 over a three year period – at a time when a laborer toiled for 25 cents an hour, if a job was available.

One of Eastham's rumrunners, Bud Cummings.

Not only was rumrunning profitable, it was also fun and relatively safe since many of those enforcing the law were not always conscientious about intercepting the flow of alcohol onto our shores. For descendants of the Mooncussers it was a pleasant and even exciting way to supplement ones income. Bud commented, "Even if I hadn't been paid I would still have done it, we had so much fun."

Only a few of the Cape Codders involved in illicit Prohibition activities were rumrunners. These lucky ones had the glamorous jobs as they rode high-powered speedboats out to Rum Row at night, picked up cases of whiskey and then evaded the slower Coast Guard vessels as they brought their cargo to shore and loaded it onto waiting trucks. Many books have been written about rumrunners and the role of the Coast Guard and other Federal officials in attempting to stifle the flow of alcohol during prohibition.[1]

I have described the Eastham rumrunning scene in my book *Growing Up On Cape Cod*. Here I would like to discuss the lesser, but still significant, involvement of the general population as revealed in Historical Society oral history interviews with Eastham citizens – the operators of fishing and quahoging boats, local entrepreneurs who dabbled in contraband goods and clam and quahog diggers who gleaned the

---

[1] *The Rum War at Sea*, the Coast Guard's official history of their battle against the rumrunners, United States Printing Office, 1964; *The Black Ships*, Everett S. Allen, Little Brown and Co., Ltd., Canada, 1965; *The Sea Fox*, the story of Manny Zora who operated out of Provincetown and was one of the best known rumrunners.

discarded bottles of alcohol from the flats and shallow waters of Cape Cod Bay.

A considerable part of the rumrunners' load was not brought directly to shore. The speedboat operator frequently arranged to transfer cases to a fishing boat, a trawler or a pleasure yacht off shore. The liquor would then be hidden under fish, bags of quahogs or seaweed and smuggled ashore by the smaller, shallow-draft vessels. Such boats were generally slower than those used by the rumrunners and fair game for the Coast Guard and Navy patrol vessels. Capture by Government officials with cases of liquor on board resulted in seizure and forfeiture of the boat. For this reason, when a Navy destroyer or Coast Guard Picket ship appeared on the horizon, the boat's captain threw overboard the contraband liquor rather than risk a fine and loss of his vessel. Cases were abandoned also when the boat's operator needed to lighten his vessel so as to free it when grounded on a sand bar or when he misjudged the tide and came too close to shore.

> **A**RT NICKERSON TELLS ABOUT COMING HOME FROM HIGH SCHOOL ONE DAY IN OCTOBER 1933 AND BEING MET BY HIS MOTHER WITH THE ORDER, "DON'T STOP NOW. GO DOWN TO SOUTH SUNKEN MEADOW. THERE'S A LOAD OF BOOZE ASHORE."

Word about such events spread through town with a velocity rivaling the speed of light. Art Nickerson tells about coming home from high school one day in October 1933 and being met by his mother with the order, "Don't stop now. Go down to South Sunken Meadow. There's a load of booze ashore." He managed to retrieve enough bottles on this particular adventure to, " – buy myself a 1931 Chevrolet Roadster and finance my Washington trip he next year."

Reminiscing with his High School classmate, Joe King, Art remembered when Coast Guard men were observing a site off a Wellfleet island where a load of cases had been dumped. He and Joe went there with a row boat, wearing foul weather gear – big bib overalls and hip boots – and equipped with a pair of garden rakes bolted in the middle like tongs or a pair of scissors. The water was so clear that they could spot the abandoned cases, in the water so long they had split and the contents were out in the open. With their homemade giant tongs they could grab the individual bottles and haul them to the surface. The Coast Guard was watching from a Patrol vessel so they couldn't bring the bottles into their skiff – the Government men would move in and seize both bottles and boat. As long as the liquor was on their person the Coast Guard could not touch them and so they stashed the contraband in their overalls or down their boots. When they got so heavy they couldn't straighten up they would waddle ashore and hide the bottles in the bush and go back for more. The Coast Guardsmen knew what they were doing, of course, and sometimes in frustration rammed their little row boat, " – not hard enough to break the boat, just enough to upset you. And they'd stand there laughing."

The Coast Guard on ships at sea played by different rules than those stationed on the shore. The former were very serious about intercepting the flow of cases of liquor and played for keeps. Equipped with machine guns and heavier armament that they were not reluctant to use, they sometimes sank a rumrunning boat, occasionally killing the operators. On the other hand, Coast Guard Stations were manned largely by local men and the Life Saving Service had only recently been integrated with the Coast Guard. These Coast Guardsmen were dedicated to saving lives rather than catching smugglers and they were not enthusiastic about having to arrest close friends.

A story, reminiscent of the English movie *Tight Little Isle*, told me by a neighbor Bud Cummings has the Federal Agents capturing over one hundred cases of whiskey. Finding all their Boston warehousing capacity full they asked Eastham's Coast Guard Captain to store the contraband in his Station's boat house for a month. When the Feds came down to Eastham to collect their cases they found only four remaining. Another of Bud's tales described a ploy he used to evade detection by the land-based Coast Guard. An anonymous tip would be phoned in to the Coast Guard, saying that a load was to be dropped at, say, Boat Meadow Creek. While the Coast Guard waited all night at Boat Meadow, the whiskey would be unloaded at Great Island in Wellfleet. The following day Bud's crew would drop off a few thank you cases at the Coast Guard Station.

An Eastham resident and Provincetown native, Lennie Tarvers, told me that his Coast Guard Captain father kept a number of five-gallon tin drums of salvaged Double Eagle Bourbon buried in their dirt floored basement. When his father was away on a several-day-long business trip, Lennie and his teenage friends dug up one tin and sampled the contents frequently, adding water to keep the level at the full mark. His father returned from his trip and found the alcoholic content of his Double Eagle closer to near beer than Bourbon. "He threw me out the door, forgetting to open the door first." Lennie also remembered that one major Provincetown dealer stored cases in an old, seldom-used warehouse. Locals quickly became aware of this practice and " – a frequent sight on the sidewalk was a little old lady pulling a four-wheeled cart holding a case of whiskey." They had learned that a loose board at the back of the warehouse allowed access and they were bringing home a "liberated" case.

An unattended case of liquor was fair game for liberators, or hijackers in less polite terms. Art and Joe routinely stored bushel bags of quahogs covered with seaweed to protect the contents on the shore for several days at a time and no one ever disturbed the shellfish. But if one case of whiskey was intermingled with the quahogs under the seaweed it wouldn't last the night. By the code of the time, taking a bag of quahogs was stealing and serious business while poaching someone's smuggled liquor was just fun and games.

Bud Cummings told of the time he was a victim of a hijacking arranged by one of the sons of Eastham's constable, Harvey Moore. The son gave Bud the friendly tip that he had overheard a state policeman telling his father that a load of booze had just been unloaded at Bud's

Nauset Road house and they intended to raid the place that night. Helped by his wife Millie and the friend, he managed to haul all the cases to pits he had dug to hold his recently harvested turnips. After covering the cases of whiskey and the turnips with layers of sand, Bud and Millie returned home at dusk and waited for the police to arrive. As dawn broke on an undisturbed night they realized that they might have been taken. They rushed back to the turnip pits and found that their informant had already disinterred and liberated a substantial portion of the hidden goods.

Repeal of the 18th Amendment in 1933 ended these escapades. Bud said it was as though an automobile assembly plant had closed down, many of the formerly busy smugglers were hanging around with nothing to do, missing the extra cash – and the excitement. Today, draggers fish-

ing for quahogs or sea clams occa-sionally find an old bottle, Log Cabin Bourbon or some other label, in their nets, a souvenir of those raffish days. Such recovered bottles are usually full with an intact cork and seal but I am told that the contents are undrinkable. After twenty or thirty years sea water seeps past the seal and ruins the liquor. Nevertheless, I've asked a quahog dragger friend who recently pulled up a bottle of Log Cabin Bourbon to let me be with him when he pulls the cork. Maybe, just maybe, this one has resisted the encroaching sea and we will be able to enjoy a sip of seventy-year-old whiskey.

Bottle of Log Cabin Bourbon, jettisoned by a rumrunner and dredged from the bottom of Cape Cod Bay in the 1900s.

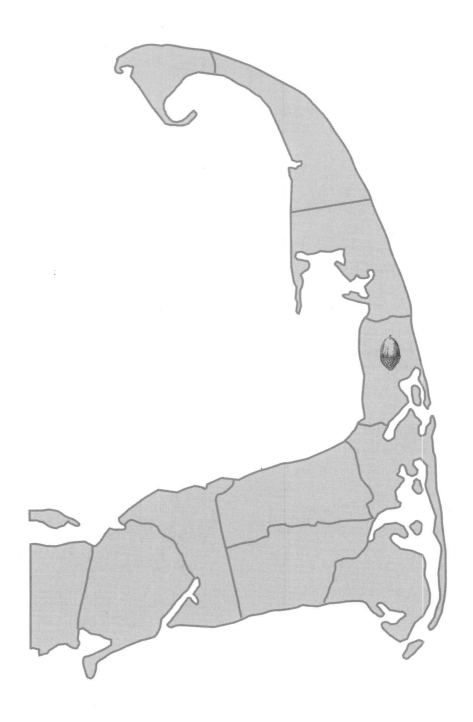

CHAPTER 16

Down to the Sea in Ships

My uncle, Captain Robert Sparrow, like many of his Cape Cod contemporaries in the early 1900s, couldn't wait to seek his fortune away from the Cape. The sea offered him the opportunity to escape the bleak future awaiting him in his home town – farming the worked-out Eastham soil or digging clams and quahogs. Graduating from Orleans High School in 1907 when 16 years old, he finished the Massachusetts Nautical Training School program two years later and started a rapid rise through the ranks as an officer on ocean-going vessels.

The Enterprise, *training vessel for the Maritime School, about 1909.*

*Cadet Robert Sparrow with classmates
at the Massachusetts Maritime
Training School, 1909*

By the time he was 23 years old he was second officer on one of the American Steamship Line vessels, the *Columbian* and he served in this capacity for two years until its final voyage in 1916.

The *Columbian* had been chartered to the French and Canada Steamship Co. and fitted to carry horses for the French Army. On her next to last voyage the *Columbian* sailed from New York for St. Nazaire in October with 1,500 horses, two vets and 65 cattle tenders who were supposed to look after the horses. The vets had been promised a bonus if they kept losses to 150 horses. In Uncle Rob's words,

We had boisterous weather and the ship was stiff and quick on rolling. The vets worked hard the first couple of days, quieting the frightened horses. They had a supply of 100 proof alcohol and injected this into the most unruly ones to calm them down. But when 150 horses had died they just gave up and went to bed for the rest of the trip, with the unused alcohol.

The ship's crew had to spend much of their time throwing the dead horses overboard; the cattle tenders were useless.

I don't know where they hired them from because they were the lowest form of man I ever saw, unclean, unshaven, always cursing.

The voyage was becoming a disaster. The reputation of the cattle tenders had preceded them. The French put armed gendarmes around the vessel to keep them on board but most managed to get ashore. The *Columbian* was supposed to leave with the rest of its convoy but had to hold up in port for an extra 24 hours to allow time to round up the missing cattle tenders. As a result the lone ship was fired on and captured by a German U-Boat not long after sailing from St. Nazaire. The U-Boat crew boarded her, removed easily transported cargo, and then the *Columbian* was torpedoed and sunk off the coast of Southern France. The Captain was held hostage and Second Officer Sparrow and his crew put in small boats.

They had to row for seven hours to reach the Spanish town of Camarinas. From there he made his way to Gibraltar and signed on as second officer on the American ship, the *Navajo*.

On his next overseas trip, in April 1917, the United States was at war with Germany. He was a deck officer (and also a recently commissioned Naval Reserve Lieutenant, J.G.), with a cargo ship, the *Dakotan*, which also carried horses. The voyage was uneventful with the Army caring for the animals and their five-vessel convoy escorted by four destroyers. But he encountered a tangle with the Army M.P.s when his ship returned to the port of Hoboken, New Jersey. They arrested him for "evading the draft." After collecting letters and affidavits to show his exemplary service he had no further trouble. In a few months he was promoted to Chief Officer on the *Dakotan* and then a year later, October 1918, at the age of 27 he had his first command position, Master of the SS *Sutherland*.

After the war he became Master of the SS *Tuckanuck*, owned by A.H. Bull Steam Ship Co. and started a 27-year involvement with the U.S.-West African shipping industry. The Bull Co., agents for the U.S. Shipping Board, operated a fleet of government-owned cargo vessels between U.S. and West African ports. For the next five years he captained ships for Bull and developed a detailed familiarity with the African trade and its ports. In view of this expertise, Bull Co. asked him to be General

Agent in charge of American vessel movements and cargo activities in West Africa, which included 57 ports from Rabat in Morocco to destinations in Angola. In this position he worked to promote the use of

The retired Captain Robert Sparrow, about 1960.

American ships in trade between Africa and America. He was quartered in Africa, Lagos, Nigeria (an area then known as the Gold Coast of Africa), and reported to A.H. Bull Steam Ship Co. and the U.S. Government Shipping Board.

His efforts resulted in a substantial improvement in the operations of the fleet and by 1928 it was in the black for the first time. Believing that the fleet offered a good opportunity for private investment, the United States Shipping Board put it up for sale. Uncle Rob moved to New York as Marine Superintendent for the winning bidder, the Barber Steam Ship Co. In addition to becoming owners of the American West Africa Line, Barber was agent for about 50 Maritime Commission vessels plying between Africa and the United States. As Marine Superintendent his duties included supervision of drydock and voyage repairs, surveying damage sustained by collisions, strandings, heavy weather, fire and other hazards. During the second World War he assisted in the conversion of vessels to carry troops, ammunition, explosives, and bulk commodity products such as oil and grain.

Most of the Maritime Commission ships and those of his employer were lost through enemy action in World War II. In 1949 Barber closed its marine operations and my uncle joined the Board of Underwriters of New York as surveyor at the port of Boston. Working for the 110 U.S. insurance company members of the Underwriter Board he was responsible for estimating hull and machinery damage repair costs, appraising vessels, carrying out salvage operations and verifying integrity and cost of repairs. Most of his work was out of the port of Boston but he also covered New Bedford, Fall River and Providence.

He finally retired in 1960, aged 69, and moved to the house he had built off Route 6, near Hemenway Landing in his home town of Eastham. After his fifty-year-long working career with enough excitement and challenges for half a dozen men, his relatives wondered how he would deal with nothing but leisure time. One of his proud boasts was that he had never spent a day without a paycheck since he left the Maritime school at the age of 19. My parents predicted that the life-long over-achieving workaholic would die of boredom within a few years. But he fooled us all, living another full, happy productive ten years. He continued his over-achieving career work habits but also he enjoyed the companionship of his new wife. They were married late in life, shortly before he retired, and moved back to Eastham.

The next chapter gives the story of the Captain's "Mate."

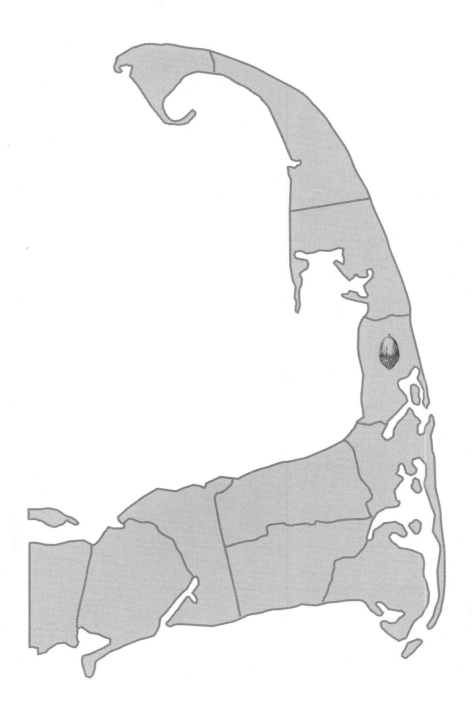

CHAPTER 17

The Captain's Mate

Uncle Rob attacked retirement with the same vigor, energy and determination he had evidenced in his 59-year-long career associated with the merchant marine industry. He was just about as busy as before but we noticed a more friendly and relaxed approach to life and attributed this to the influence of his bride of a few years, Eva Davey Sparrow. The Captain had been a bachelor up to that point. Family legend had it that in his twenties he was in love with a nurse, but she was a Catholic and neither would accept the others religious beliefs. She entered a nunnery and he remained single until Eva finally agreed to marry him. It was relatively late in life for both; they were close to 60 when wedding bells rang in 1949.

Her background was considered a bit exotic by the staid, reserved Cape Codders. She had been born on the Isle of Guernsey, took nurse's training in London, served as a Red Cross nurse stationed in the south of France during World War I, and came to Albany, New York to work in 1920. After a year in the city's hospitals she took a job as nanny for the three-year-old son of a wealthy New York City man. He had lost his wife, remarried, and the second wife didn't want to care for the baby. Eva and the child, Moncoeur Carpender, lived in an apartment with a maid, cook and chauffeur to help in caring for the "poor little rich boy." When Moncoeur grew to adolescence and no longer needed a nanny Eva lost the cushy job. After this she served in a number of New York hospitals, usually as head operating room nurse, until she and Uncle Rob married.

Captain and Mrs. Robert Sparrow, July 1969, a month before the Captain died.

Our family had known her for several years and she was not welcomed into the clan with great enthusiasm. In New York she lived in the same apartment building as the Captain, on different floors but with connecting back stairs. They had been close friends for at least twenty years and she frequently accompanied him on visits to Eastham. This didn't sit well with the Puritanical Cape Codders and many of Uncle Rob's siblings were overtly unpleasant to her, developing a scenario that pictured her as a heartless, golddigging, conniving wench. My youthful views on Eva were colored by the general air of family disapproval which prepared me to dislike her when she joined the family.

As an adult and visiting the married couple when Uncle Rob and Eva moved to Eastham, I quickly learned that the scenario was completely false. She had good jobs in New York and very much enjoyed being single in "swinging New York." He had proposed marriage many times and she only accepted when his job forced him to move to Boston. Their relationship continued to be warm and loving; they enjoyed each other's company. However, she could never forget the way she had been treated by the Sparrow family and her manner with most of us was rigidly polite, at best. My wife and I probably got to know her better than the rest of the family and even so she could be distant on occasion.

She was an attractive, trim lady with an English pink and white complexion and brown hair turning iron grey as she grew older. Fifty years or more away from the Isle of Guernsey, she retained a distinct, upper-class English accent and a strong sense of proper behavior. One morning I had neglected to shave when we called on her. She greeted us warmly, seated us in their sun room, served coffee and opened the conversation with, "You know, Donald, your Uncle Robert shaved every morning of his life."

Skewered and speechless, I remembered that I was still a member of the somewhat disreputable Sparrow clan.

No one escaped her critical eye. At Uncle Rob's funeral, one of his great-nieces wore an extremely brief mini skirt. During the post-funeral family get-together she commented to my wife, "I don't know how she avoided exposing her pubic bone."

Another black mark for the Sparrow family.

A further example of her high standards for correct behavior: Uncle Rob had brought home from Africa a lot of native artifacts including a set of bookends in the form of male and female, nude, ebony busts. There was no doubt as to the gender of the nubile female and Aunt Eva couldn't wait to get rid of the bookends after the Captain died. She asked if I wanted them and I quickly accepted saying, "Oh yes, I've always liked them." "Yes, men do," she sniffed.

Although she did have a knack for the perfect put down, most of the time she was friendly toward me and my wife and had a store of fascinating tales of her past life. She still had family on the Isle of Guernsey and wanted to see them, but she got seasick on the ocean and wouldn't fly the commercial air lines. We urged her to fly there but she was adamant; she would not step foot in a plane. We couldn't understand why, until one day she got on to her war experiences and told us,

I was in love with a French aviator when I was a Red
Cross nurse. He took me for a ride in his Jenny one day

and it was a terrible experience. There I was with the wind rushing past my face and I could see the green farmland below through a hole in the canvas under my feet. Then he did a loop-the-loop and I was almost ill. When he finally landed I was barely able to stagger away from the plane and had to have a brandy to steady my nerves. I never saw him again and I have never set foot in a plane since.

Her first winter in the States after the War she lived in a rooming house in Albany and worked in a local hospital. Reminiscing about those days, she asked,

"Have you ever heard of a man named Rickenbacker?"

"Do you mean Eddie Rickenbacker?"

"Yes, Eddie and I dated that whole winter when I first came to the U.S. He wanted to marry me and my landlord kidded me about being Mrs. Rickenbacker."

She paused and we tried to get more details about that winter in Albany. All she would say is, "Poor Eddie." No amount of coaxing would get her to elaborate and we never knew what the "Poor Eddie" meant.

After the winter in Albany she answered a newspaper ad for a nanny's position and started to take care of the "poor little rich boy." Moncoeur Carpender and the English nanny got along well and Eva had an enjoyable ten years living very comfortably with maid, cook and chauffeur to help her to care for her charge. During this period she and Uncle Rob met on a blind date when he was on vacation from his job in Africa (about 1925). He wrote to her from Africa and called when on leave again but, according to Eva, she was " – not interested, having too good a time as a single girl in New York." Once he called to say he was taking the subway to come over and see her. Her reply: "Save your nickel."

On his next trip home she agreed to go to dinner and he must have been most persuasive because they began to date.

When Moncoeur turned thirteen Eva's nanny job ended and she resumed her nursing career in New York City hospitals. Again, she managed to enjoy the New York scene. On one of our visits to her home after our Uncle died, conversation turned to those days. She told us that she and several of her co-workers frequently rented a summer cottage on Pompton Lake in New Jersey.

"We had such fun, everyone from New York would come down on week-ends. One summer Gene Tunney was there all the time. What a man he was!"

She had our attention for sure but, as with the Eddie story, she fell silent and despite our fervent pleas to elaborate, remained silent. During this time she and Uncle Rob were dating but she continued to turn down his marriage proposals. Now, we could better understand why.

After Uncle Rob's death we called on her frequently. Initially she greeted us warmly but became less receptive to visits from other members of the Sparrow family and also her husband's friends in town. Our visits fell into a pattern. I would take Deenah, her Weimaraner dog, for a walk while Reta and Eva chatted and then Eva would serve coffee in the sun room. Their aging, African parrot, Polly, was always there, standing motionless on her perch, eyes closed, featherless rump prominently displayed and holding on with her one good claw. Once she fell off, hit the bottom with a thump and lay motionless. We thought, "That's the end of Polly. What a blessing that she is gone." Minutes passed and she stirred, inched her way up the side of the cage using her beak and one claw and laboriously worked her way out to the center of the perch and resumed her motionless stance. We were puzzled that Eva didn't seem particularly concerned about the bird's plight until she finally told us its history. Uncle Rob had acquired Polly when he made a death bed promise to a close friend to always take care of the bird. He had honored his promise for 30 years and Aunt Eva kept the faith although she detested the creature.

As time went on she was less receptive to our visits and frequently antagonistic towards others. When a next door friend invited her to lunch for her birthday and brought a birthday cake, she refused the invitation and threw the cake at her. One of Uncle Rob's close friends plowed her driveway after snow storms until she accused him of damaging the roadway and asked him to stop the plowing. We attributed the odd behavior to her visibly deteriorating health.

She spurned our efforts to help and grew increasingly dependent on a middle-aged couple that had recently moved next door. We rarely saw her alone – if they were not with her when we visited they put in an appearance within two minutes. Fourteen years after the Captain's death she died from a self-administered overdose of sleeping pills, a heartbreaking end for a spirited, intelligent and feisty lady. The next door couple were the sole heirs to Uncle Rob's million dollar estate; so much for that unfriendly Sparrow family.

CHAPTER 18

Eastham "Grass"

Until the post-World War II boom, a career at sea offered one of the few opportunities for ambitious Cape Cod youths. When the first settlers arrived in 1644, Eastham was known as the "Breadbasket of Massachusetts" because of the rich, fertile layer of topsoil which had been built up as the land lay idle since the glaciers receded from the area ten thousand years ago. The "firstcomers" felled the trees and heavily farmed the area with crops of wheat and corn. Without the trees to stabilize and renew the soil it was gradually depleted. When Thoreau made one of his famous tours of the Cape in the 1849 to 57 period he described Eastham's farmland as resembling "a coarse mixture of corn meal and salt, a poor substance which gives soil a bad name."

Only a few crops were profitable in this thin, sandy ground, notable asparagus and turnips. Cranberries were grown in other Cape towns but Eastham did not have large areas of low-lying, moist, level ground required for commercial bogs. Uncle Rob (Captain Sparrow) as a boy helped work the family asparagus and turnip fields. He escaped the hard, backbreaking labor by going to sea, but his brother Dan, my father, was not as lucky. He stayed on the farm to help their widowed mother raise the younger children. His four sons had to help with the farm chores and the experiences described in the following chapters on asparagus and turnip growing catalyzed my own determination to escape the Cape.

Eastham played an important role in the cultivation of asparagus in the United States, according to Ralph Chase in one of Col. Clark's "Eastham Celebrities" interviews. By his account, an Eastham farmer obtained some seeds from France about 130 years ago and experimented with growing asparagus on his Bridge Road farm. The experiments were successful and he distributed seed to other Cape farmers. By the turn of the century a large number of asparagus farms ranging from one to twenty acres in size could be found in Eastham. A 1928 aerial photo of the Nauset to West Shore section of Eastham shows that much of the area was treeless farmland, largely in asparagus (see Chapter 20).

Not all of the farmers grew the vegetable for the market. One of my childhood friends, Art Benner, recalled that his father grew plants for sale to retailers and maintained separate beds for the State of Massachusetts Agricultural Experimental Station in Waltham. The seeds grew slender, fern-like plants the first year and Art remembered how disagreeable it was to crawl along on hands and knees as he hand weeded the delicate little things, brushing away the swarming gnat flies. At the end of the second year they plowed out the plants, pitchforked them into a Model T truck, and took them home to sort out and count by the thousand for sale to seed houses or growers.

A section of their 12-acre farm in North Eastham was set aside as an experimental plot for the Waltham Station. Here they kept a careful record of the results of varying the type of seed, amounts of fertilizer and lime, added moisture and numerous other factors. Art thought that Waltham didn't benefit greatly from the effort because varying soil conditions from one side of the bed to the other masked the effects of experimental variables. Even so, income from the Waltham Station work was considerably more financially rewarding than cutting, bunching and shipping crates of asparagus to Boston.

Eastham farmers couldn't depend of asparagus growing alone to support their families. For example, two of Eastham's largest growers were Leslie and Ralph Chase. Leslie served as Eastham's Town Clerk and Treasurer for many years and cousin Ralph served as Selectman and also operated a Real Estate company. Like his fellow farmers, my father's three acres of asparagus beds (or "grass" as he called it) provided only a portion of the family income and the entire family had to pitch in to make it a profitable enterprise. For my three brothers and myself, as well as most of our schoolmates, asparagus competed with school during the growing season – around May first to the end of June.

Our asparagus season really started as soon as the soil dried out in spring and we could chop off the dried ferns at ground level with a hoe. Father pulled the four to six foot, grayish brown stalks into huge piles with a hay rake and then set them on fire. The dry, brittle fern residues burned quickly and the bright orange, roaring bonfires lasted only a short while. The piles usually sat in the field for a few days and I remember the rabbits hiding in the piles came sprinting out as the fires spread.

Next, preparing the beds for the growing season, we spread commercial limestone to replace the crushed clam and quahog shells early settlers used to combat the acidity of the Cape soil. The plant also seemed to thrive on the salt from the seaweed which we harrowed into the soil to provide humus. This worked out well for us too because we were able to use the three-foot deep pile of seaweed which father had placed around our kitchen foundation in the fall to provide badly needed insulation. A dressing of manure followed by a double, right and left, bladed plow to hill up each row to a height of eight to ten inches completed the spring-time asparagus chores. We were ready for warm weather.

The first stalks appeared around the first of May and from then until July Fourth my three brothers and I got up every morning at dawn to cut asparagus. Typically it took two hours for the crew of father and his four sons, plus a hired hand, to finish the daily cut and bring the "grass" to

The Sparrow family cutting asparagus, Uncle Dan's Pond in the background.

the barn for bunching. The picture of the family at work bears out part of Mr. Chase's comment that all a good asparagus cutter needed was, "a strong back and a weak mind." We walked the rows bent at a 90 degree angle, straightening only to lay a handful of asparagus, sharpen our knife, or swat gnat flies. The knife, a seven inch long rectangle at the start of the season, was only three or four inches long come July Fourth due to the frequent sharpening of its square end.

The picture was taken on the last of the three beds that we cut every morning. Mother started the breakfast bacon frying as soon as she spotted us from the kitchen window across the pond. The aroma floating over the water's surface drove us mad as we rushed to complete the cut and get to the breakfast table. Our morning meal started with cereal and cut fruit lathered with heavy cream, followed by bacon and eggs, the whites set by spooning the hot bacon grease over them. Homemade bread, butter and jam accompanied the bacon and eggs, all washed down with Ovalteen or Postum. Thus fortified we felt ready to take on school.

After breakfast mother and a hired hand bunched the day's cut. She told me once that she spent her spring mornings operating a bunching treadle with one foot and rocking a cradle with the other. The bunched product was attractive, three inches by ten, perfectly symmetrical with the tips curved inward, dark green at the tip shading to pale green at the bottom with a touch of white at the ends and held together with two circles of bright red ribbon.

Six days a week we shipped five to twenty crates of asparagus to Faneuil Hall market in Boston. For many years Eastham farmers took their crates to the Depot for transport to Boston, but by the 1930s trucks were replacing the train and Hemingway's Transport truck picked up our daily shipment every evening. Father had a stock of shipping tags for the various produce houses in Faneuil Market and studied the checks in his daily mail so as to pick the firm getting the best prices. The most succulent stalks he put aside for the Somerset Club, an exclusive men's club in Boston. They paid top price, five dollars for a crate of 24 bunches, each bunch made up of stalks at least one inch in diameter. In father's words they were, "as big as my thumb," and he had massive, work hardened hands.

> **A**S WE CRAWLED THROUGH THE MUGGY, AIRLESS VEGETATION, STRIPPED TO THE WAIST AND BATTLING GREENHEAD AND FLAT IRON FLIES WE DREAMED OF THE COOL WATERS OF MINISTERS POND OR THE ATLANTIC OCEAN AT NAUSET BEACH.

Another asparagus chore was the preparation of a home-made insecticide used to control the insect pests which disfigured and lowered the market value of asparagus. We mixed a lethal combination of bran mash, molasses, ground up citrus fruits and a copper-arsenic salt known as Paris Green. Bugs disappeared quickly after we hand-spread the crumbly mixture on the growing stalks. Mother insisted on a thorough hand washing after this duty and we assumed that customers rinsed their vegetables before cooking.

Fourth of July was greeted with wild enthusiasm. There was no more early morning duty and – there were fire crackers! But, we couldn't really relax too much; asparagus required our constant attention. When cutting stopped the stalks grew to form six foot high ferns. Weeds were controlled by a cultivator pulled by our broad-backed horse, Jerry. We rode bare back with our legs sticking out almost horizontally. When the ferns became too thick to allow Jerry between the rows we had to weed by hand. As we crawled through the muggy, airless vegetation, stripped to the waist and battling greenhead and flat iron flies we dreamed of the cool waters of Ministers Pond or the Atlantic Ocean at Nauset Beach.

When his beds were about 20 years old and too aged for good commercial production father turned them over to one of us boys. We became young, enthusiastic (initially), entrepreneurs, cutting, bunching, crating and shipping to market. Our products went to one of a half dozen Faneuil Hall merchants and we agonized over the decision as to which one to favor with our business. It was hard work and the rewards were meager. The old beds grew skinny, "shoelace" stalks which brought little more than two dollars a crate. Getting an education to enable us to seek our fortune across the bridge became more and more attractive.

The three asparagus beds on the Sparrow farm were the last my father installed; the off-Cape competition was becoming too strong. First from New Jersey "grass" in the early 1900s and then later from the Carolinas. Mr. Chase and others formed the Eastham Farmer's Association to combat these outside threats. Their logo marked an early use of Nauset Light as an advertising asset. Finally, the introduction of refrigerated rail cars opened the door to asparagus from West Coast growers. The Association closed down in 1935 and no new beds were set in Eastham after that. Now we find an occasional single asparagus stalk in our fields, a survivor from one of father Sparrow's "grass" beds.

CHAPTER 19

A Tribute to the Noble Turnip

Eastham turnips are, uncontestably, the best in the world. I am convinced of this as are all Eastham residents as well as visitors who are fortunate enough to sample this delectable dish. It is true that not everyone in America feels this way. In my youth I could never understand why. Mammy Yokum's "preserved turnips" in Al Capp's comic strip *Li'l Abner* were supposed to be an example of a ridiculous, unpalatable yokel food. To me they sounded mighty good, if prepared from the Eastham variety of turnip, and I waited for Al Capp to supply the recipe. Only when I left home and experienced the off-Cape version of this vegetable did I grasp the humor in someone serving "preserved" turnips, non-Eastham of course.

Our mother didn't make preserved turnips, she just peeled, boiled, mashed and added lots of butter. It was always the star accompaniment to our Thanksgiving turkey. The rutabaga or yellow turnip had no place on our holiday table; we had to serve the white, Eastham variety. The real McCoy has a pale lavender top and a pure white body.

The flesh is also a snowy white and, when cooked, smooth, free of fibers and delicately flavored.

But why do Eastham turnips taste so much better than those grown anywhere else? Could it be a special seed, or some trace element in Eastham soil or the unique combination of temperature, humidity, pH and salinity found in our town's soil, or could it be a secret ingredient used by Eastham farmers such as Art Nickerson and Raymond Brackett? Nobody can give me a logical answer although I lean in the direction of a trace element found only in the outwash plains of the outer Cape. After all, our soil is a mish-mash of a wide variety of materials scooped up by the glacier advancing over thousands of miles of Canadian landscape 10,000 years ago. It's possible that one special substance could have been picked up from some remote area, Baffin Land or Hudson Bay for example, and deposited where Eastham was formed as the glacier ground to a halt on the coast of this continent, melted and then retreated back to the Arctic. Whatever the reason, we should give thanks for the combination of events which led to the existence of the noble Eastham turnip.

> **W**E HAD TO SERVE THE WHITE, EASTHAM VARIETY. THE REAL MCCOY HAS A PALE LAVENDER TOP AND A PURE WHITE BODY. THE FLESH IS ALSO A SNOWY WHITE AND, WHEN COOKED, SMOOTH, FREE OF FIBERS AND DELICATELY FLAVORED.

One of the events associated with the celebration of Eastham's Tercentenary illustrates the long-standing importance of the vegetable to the town. In the fall of 1951 more than 50 men participated in a festival-like event, a turnip pull on the Harry Collins' farm. Mr. Collins was ill and his friends helped him by pulling, trimming and storing 1,300 bushels of choice Eastham turnips on his farm off Bridge Road. Members of the Grange and Odd Fellows Lodges invaded his turnip fields and spent the day harvesting the crop. Work halted at noon and the volunteers adjourned to the Town Hall where women of the Eastham Grange served quahog chowder, apple pie and coffee to the hungry workers.

Among the volunteers was George Nickerson, a North Eastham turnip grower and the father of Art Nickerson, Eastham's reigning Mr. Turnip. Art, who is well past 80, is still growing them despite some physical problems over the last few years. Last year he grew enough for his wife, Marcia, to have turnips on the dinner table for 45 days and also sell some at Eastham's Superette and Phoenix Fruit and Vegetable in Orleans.

Another Eastham native, Art Benner, remembered how they got the seed for their Eastham turnips. The tops of turnips which had wintered over in sand and seaweed-covered pits were lopped off and planted in the spring. They took root, grew foliage with yellow blossoms which formed seeds. When dried, "you could cut them off with a sickle, thresh them out in a flour barrel, winnow all the chaff out, it was like small bird shot and that was your seed." One pound was sufficient to plant an acre of turnips, according to Art Nickerson.

During the Depression, turnip growing was something of a gamble. Art told of shipping out a lot of turnips to the Boston market and not realizing enough on the sale to cover the freight. "They'd get a bill for the freight, if you can imagine that. Sometimes they wouldn't even unload, just dump them, you know. That means all your work and time and expense, fertilizer, is down the drain."

Nowadays the situation is quite different. Only a few farmers grow turnips and the demand is such that one is lucky to find the real thing in the stores. When I retired to Eastham close to 20 years ago, the supply of these turnips was already a little tight. I decided to buy a bushel and store them in a cool but not freezing place so that we could enjoy them all winter long. At that time Mr. Raymond Brackett in North Eastham, nephew of the owner of Sam Brackett's General Store, was one of the largest growers. I called and inquired about the availability of a quantity of his prized turnips. He hemmed and hawed and finally asked, "Was your father Dan Sparrow?" "Why yes, he was." "Well, I don't think I'll even have enough for my regular customers."

I begged and pleaded but to no use, he didn't have any Eastham turnips for a Sparrow. Later I learned from a longtime friend that my father and Raymond had words 50 years ago. Fortunately, Eastham turnips grown by Art Nickerson were, and still are, available in the local stores.

CHAPTER 20

Cedar Bank Links

*I*n the late 1920s some of Eastham's asparagus and turnip fields were converted to an 18-hole, private golf course. It was private in the sense that only one person, and his guests, played the course. In 1925 a wealthy Boston and North Shore resident, Quincy Adams Shaw, came to Eastham to plan and build what was to become Cedar Bank Links. He acquired the necessary land and over the next three years laid out the course and, assisted by local workers, constructed an 18-hole "links," the Scottish term for a golf course. He was able to indulge his hobby because his father had been one of the developers of the Calumet Copper Mines in Upper Peninsula Michigan. These mines held deposits of electrolytically pure copper and Calumet was the source of a number of Boston family fortunes.

Mr. Shaw utilized the existing terrain in designing his links, the only earth-moving equipment was an iron scoop pulled by my father's horse, Jerry. The course bordered a number of bodies of water – Salt Pond, Nauset Marsh and several fresh water ponds. Nauset

Indian tribes lived and hunted near water because of the abundant supply of game birds and animals attracted by the water and the readily available fish and shellfish. While digging bunkers (traps), my father

uncovered large quantities of Indian artifacts including a stone, corn grinding pestle and, literally, thousands of arrowheads. A 1928 aerial photo taken when the construction was just completed in 1928 shows asparagus and turnip field furrows in many of the fairways.

Mr. Quincy Adams Shaw before the fireplace in Cedar Bank Links clubhouse.

A schematic diagram of Cedar Bank illustrates the proximity of the course to water hazards. One of the most diabolic holes was the 150-yard number 11 where the player had to drive over Salt Pond Inlet.

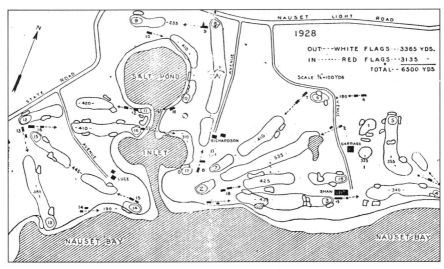

Layout of Mr. Shaw's golf course.

Aerial view of the "links."

Players hauled themselves and their caddies across the river and back in a scow equipped with ropes and pulleys. The river (as we called it) exerted an almost hypnotic attraction and a large percentage of the drives ended up in the drink, including mine when I played the course as a teenaged golfer (my father was the caretaker and allowed us to play on weekdays). Equally cruel was the 17th hole, coming back, across the river. It was a medium, dogleg-to-the-right hole (only 250 yards), but the drive had to clear the stream and also avoid a large salt marsh which bordered the fairway and green.

WEEKEND GUESTS INCLUDED FRANCIS OUIMET, ONE OF THE UNITED STATES' EARLY GOLF CHAMPIONS, WHO HELPED MR. SHAW DESIGN THE COURSE AND, ON ONE MEMORABLE WEEKEND, BOBBY JONES PLAYED THE LINKS.

When the Links was finished in 1928 the *Boston Transcript* (now defunct but then Boston's leading newspaper) did a story on it and found that it had "one of the finest natural

Mr. Shaw with guests Francis Ouimet, Bobby Jones and Rodney Brown, about 1932.

layouts in the world." Weekend guests included Francis Ouimet, one of the United States' early golf champions, who helped Mr. Shaw design the course and, on one memorable weekend, Bobby Jones played the links.

The 1930's Depression overlapped the heyday of Cedar Bank Links and Mr. Shaw's hobby gave a much needed shot in the arm to Eastham's economy during that difficult period. The course and clubhouse employed a staff of about 10 and Mr. Shaw's parties of 15 to 20 friends every weekend during the golfing season (roughly April to October) added significantly to the town's cash flow. One of prohibition's rum-runners was on permanent retainer with Mr. Shaw. In addition, Mr. Shaw often instructed his chauffeur to buy shoes and clothing for those school students whom the Eastham Grammar School Principal indicated were in need of help. He also gave financial support to Eastham youths who wished to go to college (I was one).

After the War, Mr. Shaw, in his early eighties and failing health, began to lose interest in his plaything and by 1950 it was no longer being maintained as a playable course. Fairways and greens disappeared as cedar trees, bayberry bushes and other natural, wild growth took over. Most of the acreage was within the Cape Cod National Seashore boundaries and the ingrowth has been allowed to continue. It is hard to imagine, looking at a 1988 aerial photo taken from the same spot as the 1928 picture, that Cedar Bank ever existed.

Nauset Marsh trail maintained by the Seashore traverses some of the old course. Present-day users of the Trail can find places where my father dug bunkers with Jerry and the iron scoop and a concrete roller used to level the playing surface of greens rests next to the old number three fairway, bordering Nauset Marsh. My wife and I take the Nauset Marsh walk at least once a week and recently she found an old golf ball partially buried in the mulch where the trail goes near the salt marsh. Only one half of the cover was intact and it was badly discolored. We made the mistake of placing it in a desk drawer where it dried out over

Aerial view of Cedar Bank 60 years after the 1928 photo.

the space of several weeks. When we showed our treasure to a friend it looked as though it had exploded. The shriveled cover had slipped off and the tightly wound elastic strand had fractured in so many pieces the ball appeared to be covered with rubber fuzz. We are convinced that it was an authentic 1930s Cedar Bank ball. If any one walking the Nauset Marsh Trail is lucky enough to find another one, keep your treasure in a moist environment, and please call me.

CHAPTER 21

Shopping -
Past, Present,
and Future

Taking care of Cedar Bank Links, along with a number of other jobs, kept my mother and father working at a feverish pitch. My mother was kept busy because she had to line up caddies for the golfers, provide milk, cream and eggs for the Shaw cook, handle messages for the guests, be on the alert for Cedar Bank guests who came to use our phone (Mr. Shaw didn't like phones in his clubhouse), and help with the monthly golf course accounts in addition to bunching asparagus every day in the spring and taking care of the house and four boys. Fortunately she didn't have to spend time away from the house to do the family shopping; the tradesmen came to us. At least once a week merchants came to our home to sell groceries, fish, meats and even patent medicines. The system worked well. Mother had a chance to inspect the merchandise while exchanging the latest gossip with the sales person.

Suppliers of house furnishings, furniture, clothing and other non-consumables didn't come to the homes. For these items we resorted to one of our two "bibles" – the Sears

Roebuck or Montgomery Ward catalogs. In the heyday of these two mail-order giants we could buy anything we needed by studying the catalog, making our choice, filling out an order form and putting it in the mail. "Anything" is not too strong a word to characterize the enormous range of products and services available – one could buy household appliances, farming equipment, works of art, non-prescription drugs, toys, a house, an automobile – literally anything.

Of course we didn't send off an order every week. Mother usually put together a big order every two months or so. Making our selection for these shopping orgies, especially the spring and fall clothing order or Christmas gifts was a serious business. When the eagerly awaited Parcel Post package arrived we inspected, tried on, tested, felt, and hefted the merchandise. All too frequently we had to return something – it didn't fit or was the wrong color or we didn't like the styling or it was something we hadn't ordered. And, we had to pay the postage to mail it back to "Sears and Sendback" or "Monkey Ward."

Shopping practices after the War went through radical, evolutionary changes. Supermarkets appeared in just about all the communities of any size and there was no need for merchants to make house calls. Shopping malls grew like Topsy and general catalog sales faltered and then died. Sears built stores in malls and survived while Wards dithered for a long while and finally declared bankruptcy in the year 2001.

In the waning years of the 20th century we saw further evolutionary changes in the way people shop. Specialty catalog marketing grew to the point where postal employees have difficulty stuffing all the sales magazines into my post office box. The crush peaks at Christmas time but all through the year the U.S. Postal Service delivers such tempting offerings as clothing, hardware, jewelry, fruits, candy, and packaged travel tours – it's hard to imagine any service or object smaller than a dog house that cannot be purchased from a catalog.

More recently we have Internet shopping. Log on, locate the website of a marketer, click on a product you want to buy, type in your credit card number and UPS deliver a package to your door. The growth of the number of Internet companies carrying every imaginable product and service reached chain reaction proportions in the last half of the 1990s. Companies such as Amazon.com, eBay and Yahoo made paper millionaires of thousands of entrepreneurs, although most of the companies have yet to make a profit. In the millennium year of 2000 many of these companies folded or needed to sharply lower their expectations. No one knows, including me, if this is symptomatic of a basic flaw in this marketing approach. Resumption of the 1990s explosive growth of E. shopping could put a big dent in the existing shopping malls future potential and we all should be buying Amazon.com stock. If the current slow growth continues, you might be advised to hold on to your WalMart stock.

> **A** VIEWER AT HOME COULD TASTE THE BEER, SELL THE PERFUME, SAVOR THE GIANT BURGER, FEEL THE FIT AND FABRIC QUALITY OF CLOTHING.

I'll admit to a belief that the future of specialty catalogs and E. shopping is cloudy because the buyer cannot inspect the merchandise before ordering. Returns will cut into profits and could be uneconomically high. Thinking about this problem, I remembered Aldous Huxley's grim novel about a possible, science-based future, *Brave New World*, published in 1932. One of the author's imaginings intrigued me. A technical development called "Feelies" made it possible for a movie goer, or television viewer, to experience the physical reactions of the actors on the screen, or tube. If an actor were embracing Sophia Loren, for example, every male in the audience would feel all the sensations of actually clutching the actress and, presumably, women would experience Sophia's reactions.

The concept was similar to Virtual Reality but with all the senses in play – taste, smell and touch in addition to sight and hearing. With this development the E. shopping service would be able to demonstrate every aspect of the product on sale. A viewer at home could taste the beer, sell the perfume, savor the giant burger, feel the fit and fabric quality of clothing. The rate of product returns should drop dramatically. Goodbye specialty catalogs and so long shopping malls.

One of my stepsons agrees that the device has great commercial potential. We plan to go public soon with FEELIES.COM and we expect that shareholders will become rich beyond the dreams of avarice. Now, Jeff, if I can just work out a few technical details....

CHAPTER 22

Our Once Great American Sport

My parents rarely took time off from work. A week-long autumn auto trip every three or four years and a trip to the Chicago World's Fair in 1933 was about it for vacations. I don't remember them ever going to a movie or a sports event. Growing up in this environment, their four sons also rarely indulged in such frivolous pursuits. We did play at baseball a lot, mostly backyard, pick-up games, usually with fewer than a full complement of nine players per side. We followed baseball's big league games avidly and had to endure the "silly season," when there was no solid sports news from the last of the World Series games to the start of baseball spring training. Sports writers had to invent contract disputes and sore-armed star pitchers and speculated endlessly on the chances of their favorite players and teams in the upcoming season.

The first of March freed them from the straitjacket; finally the teams were allowed to open up their Florida spring training camps, and there was real news to report. Baseball fans were equally elated when March 1 rolled around. The teams that my friends and I supported, the Boston Red Sox and the Boston Braves, were never far from our minds and we couldn't wait to see how they would fare this year. The two teams were as unlike as night and day. The mighty Red Sox were run by their affluent owner, Tom Yawkey who could afford to buy the Leagues' greatest stars in his eternally frustrated quest for a World Series pennant. Shortstop Joe Cronin (the player-manager) and pitcher Lefty Grove were brought in to ensure a pennant, to no avail. Mighty slugger Jimmy Foxx and catcher Mickey Cochrane came from Connie Mac's lowly, and broke, Phillies – no pennant. Yawkey loaded the roster with stars purchased from other big league teams – Bobby Doer, Doc Cramer, Heinie Manush, Dom DiMaggio, and Jim Tabor, but the pennant eluded him, the October flag pole was always bare.

The Braves were another story: close to bankruptcy, usually in last place and with a squad made up of over-the-hill players, stars-to-be and run-of-the-mill work horses. Rabbit Maranville with his over the shoulder, vest pocket catches, "poosh-em-up" Tony Cuccinello, Wally Berger, Sibby Sisti, were some of the names that Braves fans had to learn to love. In 1936, the owner, Judge Fuchs, changed the team name to the Boston Bees in what seemed, even then, a misguided effort to create a more vital image for the team. His experiment lasted for all of six months. At about the same time the Judge hired an aging ex-Red Sox and then Yankee star, Babe Ruth, to punch up the fans' interest. He hit a few home runs, but the team couldn't afford his cavalier approach to outfield play and he faded into retirement. We didn't expect much from the Braves/Bees and they rarely lived up to even our minuscule expectations.

We followed the fortunes of the two teams avidly, never missing a chance to listen to the broadcasts on our Atwater-Kent radio earphones. Fred Hooey gave us the play-by-play account live for home games and recreated away games from the summary of the action telegraphed to him. As President Reagan revealed when he discussed his early career as a sports announcer, the away games required considerable imagination on the part of the broadcaster. The clatter of the telegraph key in the background showed that Fred was just relaying what he could decipher from the dots and dashes, but the sound seemed to add excitement to his narration. The programs were sponsored by Wheaties, with their star salesman, Jack Armstrong, "the All-American Boy." The best player in my set, Whit Howes, served a bowl of the cereal when we listened to the game at his house, and I recall solemnly eating my Wheaties while following Fred's account of the action.

We could hardly wait for the mail to bring us the *Boston Post* to read the details of all the daily games. Their sports cartoonist, Bob Coyne, drew stylized caricatures for each of the teams. A Red Sox player was a sartorially elegant dude and an American Indian with war paint, feathers, head dress and tomahawk represented a Boston Brave. The Brooklyn Dodgers were depicted as the dirtiest, most slovenly bums, husbanding the stub of a tattered cigar, worldly effects in bandana handkerchiefs tied to a pole slung over their shoulders and both shoes worn through to their socks. The Washington Senators were carpet-bagger politicians, watch chain stretched across an expansive, vest-clad stomach, striped pants, long silvery hair topped by a black slouch hat. The Yankees, his and our special enemy, were effete dandies in elegant pin stripes and a smug smile.

> **B**OB COYNE, DREW STYLIZED CARICATURES FOR EACH OF THE TEAMS. A RED SOX PLAYER WAS A SARTORIALLY ELEGANT DUDE AND AN AMERICAN INDIAN WITH WAR PAINT, FEATHERS, HEAD DRESS AND TOMAHAWK REPRESENTED A BOSTON BRAVE.

But the Yankees were far from effete. Every year the Sox and the Yanks were locked in a no-holds-barred, knock-down, no-captives battle. The two teams were even-up til the middle of August. Then they had a crucial, five-game series and the Sox would break our hearts, dropping four out of five, allowing the Yanks to cruise along to the pennant and World Championship.

When not listening to or reading about the major league teams, we were out playing baseball or watching the homegrown version. We played catch after school, pickup games in the cow pasture, sandlot ball and during school recess. A few of the locals went to the Minor Leagues, but failed to make it to the top. One Orleans semi-pro from away, Johnny Brocoa, went on to pitch for the Yankees. He married the sister of one of my high school classmates, and how we envied him.

We dreamed of seeing a Major League game. One year a summer visitor family invited several neighborhood teenagers to a Cleveland-Red Sox game. We were in box seats, directly in back of the Sox dugout, with an unobstructed view of our heroes. We watched Jimmy Foxx with his massive biceps, squeezing the bat so hard we thought sawdust would flow out of the end, Dom DiMaggio's catlike grace as he loped to his outfield position, Bobby Doer and Joe Cronin working together on an effortless double play. They seemed invincible, but the team managed to disappoint us again. Cleveland's shortstop, Lou Boudreau, had a hot day, hitting four hard, clothes-line, two-baggers off the infamous left field wall and the Indians beat us.

In those days I could name most of the players, knew the batting averages, won-lost data on every major league team, and the standing of the teams. Now baseball competes with many other professional sports for the fan's attention. Instead of the January to March "silly season" we have a continuous silly season with overlapping accounts of baseball, basketball, college and professional football, hockey, golf and tennis. Stories of the marital transgressions of some players, their problems with the narcotics authorities and the latest entrants to the $100 million dollar club fill the sports pages. But I get confused, are they baseball or football or basketball or hockey or golf or mud wrestling stars – and do I really care?

CHAPTER 23

Radio Before Television

*T*he first radio broadcasting license was issued by the U.S. Department of Commerce in 1921, the year I was born. It might be said that radio and I grew up together, although broadcasting grew a lot faster, and a lot wealthier, than I did. Radio showed early, explosive growth and by 1927 there were thirteen million radio sets in use in the United States.

One of these was my parents first radio, a black box, battery-powered Atwater Kent with earphones. The driving force for the sale of radio receivers in those days was sports broadcasting and this along with weather reports, were the two main uses of our set. I remember fighting my three brothers for one of the two pair of earphones so that I could listen to Fred Hoey describing a Boston Red Sox or Boston Braves baseball game.

Weather variations were important to my father in both of his roles, farmer and golf course supervisor, and we tuned in the weather report every morning. After the earphones had been replaced by a set with a large loud-speaker horn we could all hear the gruff, monotone voice of WEEI weather forecaster, E. C. Rideout, telling us when to expect a frost in low-lying areas.

During the early days of broadcast radio, a common Christmas gift for young boys was a kit with the components of a crystal radio set. By assembling the antennae, battery, earphones, crystal and "cat's whisker" feeler, it was possible to receive broadcast programs. The radio was tuned by moving the feeler over the surface of the crystal, the position on the surface determining which program came through the earphones. I never understood the principle behind the device and never became adept in operating one, but some of my friends spent long hours moving the whisker over the crystal and telling me, "I pulled in KDKA in Pittsburgh last night" or, "I can get WBZ in Boston any time I want."

Crystal sets couldn't compete with radios built with a different technology, featuring multiple glass vacuum tubes. Our Atwater Kent was one of these much more reliable and tunable receivers. After several years the black box with its ungainly horn was replaced by an impressive Motorola console model, powered by house current, housed in a three-foot-high, simulated mahogany case with a built-in loud speaker. The new Motorola stood in the living room beside father's wooden rocking chair and a floor lamp with a beaded fringe shade. This was our "entertainment center."

The hours of three to six, after school and before dinner, were devoted to the juvenile adventure stories such as Jack Armstrong – the All American Boy, Dick Tracy and Little Orphan Annie. Sponsors of these shows tended to be cereal companies. We saved the Wheaties, Ralston Purina, and Shredded Wheat box tops, mailed them off for prizes and then waited for what seemed eternities for the mail to deliver our secret code ring, magic trick or official Dick Tracy police badge.

Beginning when I was eight years old, the family gathered around the radio after supper every evening to listen to two white performers playing black character in "The Amos 'n Andy Show." The program became the most popular show on radio – it was claimed that President Roosevelt would not schedule any meetings when Amos 'n Andy were on the air. My parents and their four sons were glued to the set, seven to seven fifteen, Monday to Friday as the two men created a comedy show with scores of black and white characters. Wildly popular for the next ten years or so, this unfortunate comedy wouldn't have lasted a week in today's social and political environment. The black people were depicted as somewhat lazy, shiftless and generally irresponsible. The show probably delayed the integration of blacks into the American scene by at least twenty years.

Sometimes, if we had finished our homework we were allowed to stay up and listen to the news. H. V. Kaltenborn was one of the earliest and sort of pompous, we thought. Lowell Thomas was lots more interesting, especially his adventure stories and we also liked "The March of Time" with its voice of doom "Time – Marches – On." We were always allowed to stay up to hear President Franklin D. Roosevelt give one of his Fireside Chats and even in our staunchly Republican household, felt reassured by his calm, confident voice.

"SUSPENSE" OR "THE INNER SANCTUM" WITH ITS TRADEMARK OPENER, THE LONG, DRAWN-OUT SOUND OF A CREAKING DOOR. OUR SPECIAL FAVORITE WAS "THE SHADOW" – "WHAT EVIL LURKS IN THE HEARTS OF MANKIND? THE SHADOW KNOWS," AND THEN A SINISTER CACKLE.

We couldn't get enough of the Lindbergh baby kidnap story in 1932 or accounts of the capture and trial of the kidnapper, Bruno Hauptmann in 1935. Another radio news reporter, Gabriel Heater, skyrocketed to fame when he broadcast the execution of Hauptmann and filled the air for a whole hour when the announced time for the electrocution was pushed back. He had no script, everything he said was ad libbed.

Homework finished, we sometimes were allowed to listen to the mystery shows later in the evening such as "Suspense" or "The Inner Sanctum" with its trademark opener, the long, drawn-out sound of a creaking door. Our special favorite was "The Shadow" – "What evil lurks in the hearts of mankind? The Shadow knows," and then a sinister cackle. We tried to be as suave as the dapper, man-about-town Lamont Cranston, who turned into the implacable enemy of criminals when faced with their dastardly deeds.

In the middle 1930s vaudeville performers started to move into broadcast radio. Comedians such as Fibber Magee and Molly, Ed Wynn, Fred Allen and Jack Benny became our Sunday night stand-standbys. Of course we couldn't see them so they all had gimmicks to differentiate themselves from their competition. Some of these were The Perfect Fool, Ed Wynn; the miser Jack Benny with his creaking bank vault door when he needed pocket money; and Fred Allen with his Allen's Alley Players featuring the perky, opinionated Mrs. Nussbaum. A popular script device was a continuing, week-to-week joke – pinch-penny Jack Benny clinging to his ancient Maxwell auto and Fibber Magee opening his filled-to-overflowing closet with a resulting cacophony of sounds as the contents cascaded out and crashed to the floor.

My brothers and I couldn't be bothered with the soap box operas and mother never had the time for such nonsense. However, we heard enough of them to know that music was important in setting the mood in these daytime dramas. Organ music swelling up at the start or during an episode of "Ma Perkins," "Helen Trent" or "Just Plain Bill" could be threatening, ominous, lighthearted, frivolous, poignant, serious, sad; whatever emotion the daily script was trying to convey.

Sound effects in addition to music were important in all radio broadcasts. When our High School class went on its Washington trip in 1937, the highlight of our New York stopover was a Radio City Studio tour. We learned that the sound of a raging forest fire can be simulated by crunching a sheet of cellophane next to the microphone and the sound of a horse could be duplicated by clopping two coconut shells on a plank for cantering across a bridge or with a velvet drape on the plank for trotting on turf.

As we grew older and grew interested in popular music, the "Lucky Strike Hit Parade" became our favorite evening program. Featuring the ten top hit tunes of the week, the performers had to find new ways of presenting songs that stayed among the top ten week after week after week. I remember two of the artists, the lovely and talented Giselle McKensie who played the violin as well as warbling the tunes and a male singer with the improbable name of Snooky Lansom.

One of radio's most memorable events came in 1938 when Orson Welles on his "Mercury Theatre" show presented his version of H. G. Wells, "War of the Worlds," in which Martians invaded and started to take over the United States. Although it was introduced as a science fiction drama and concerned listeners had only to go through the dial and find normal programming everywhere else, the broadcast created havoc in some of the supposed invasion areas of New Jersey and New York. Streets were clogged with fleeing people. The 21-year-old theatrical genius, Orson Welles, became an overnight celebrity.

I had just left Eastham to go away to school and, not having a radio in my dormitory room, didn't hear the show. I don't know how I might have reacted. I'm pleased, although not very surprised, to report that Eastham radio listeners accepted the show for what it was, science fiction, and did not grab pitchforks and rush into the night to repel the alien invaders.

The show has become a radio classic and has been rebroadcast numerous times in the U.S. and in translated versions overseas. My wife was living near Paris in the small suburban town of St. Sauveur when a French version of "The War of the Worlds" was broadcast in 1939. She reports that the residents reacted the same way the New Jersey citizens had the year before; many of them panicked and took to the streets to escape the evil Martians.

After World War II and then the coming of television, radio went through a complete metamorphosis. Now it is useful mainly for background music, spot news and weather reports and a multitude of talk shows. There seems to be no limit to the public's appetite for radio hosts who are willing to discuss any number of subjects with views ranging from far right conservative to slightly left of center and, it seems to me, the more salacious, scurrilous or scatological the better. The people who support these shows could be direct descendants of those who lost their cool when Welles aired "The War of the Worlds" in 1938. They will believe anything that comes over the airways without bothering to check the validity or even rationality of what they hear.

CHAPTER 24

Silver Screen

We could maintain contact with big league baseball via the radio, but to make the five-mile trip to the Orleans Theatre we needed wheels. Before any of my three brothers and I were old enough to drive a car, this was close to impossible; our folks weren't movie goers. Even when Wilbur turned sixteen and got his license, wrestling car permission from father required a lot of wheedling, begging and tears.

A replay of an old Harold Lloyd film on TV recently brought me back to one of he first times we were able to go to the Orleans movie house. As the comedian with his trademark, horn-rimmed glasses hung from a huge clock, suspended 25 stories above Times Square, clinging desperately to the moving minute hand as it approached the half hour, I grew misty eyed remembering the long gone movie house. It occupied the first floor of a large wooden building called the Snow Block on Main Street next to a small Post Office (now the home of an art gallery) and the cemetery in the center of Orleans. Movies were shown there from the early 1920s until

The Snow Block with Orleans Theatre entrance on the left.

1938 when the cinema moved to a new, brick building, now the site of the CVS pharmacy.

The Wilcox family owned and operated the Orleans Theatre for most of its existence. Chris and Bertha Wilcox and their three children moved from New Bedford early in the first decade of the twentieth century to manage a chicken farm in Eastham. Chris was a licensed movie projector operator and moonlighted as projectionist for the owner of movie theaters in Wellfleet and Orleans. He bought the business, including the theater building in 1922, ran both movie houses for a few years and then closed the Wellfleet theater to concentrate on Orleans. The family which had grown from three to seven children since coming to the Cape, moved to Orleans in 1924. Two of them, Mary and Christine (now Mrs. Gardiner Munsey and Mrs. Robert Williams), live in Orleans and they and their husbands have been kind enough to spend time reminiscing with me about the pre-war days of the Orleans Theatre.

The building Chris bought, formerly owned by Harry Snow, was a three-story wooden building with the theatre on the ground floor and on the upper levels a large auditorium used for dances and high school basketball games plus living quarters.

It had been built in 1895 by Captain Aaron Snow, Harry's grandfather, and it held, at various times, meeting rooms, a gymnasium, an enclosed shooting gallery and a livery stable as well as the above-mentioned activities. For many years it had been the social center of Orleans.

By 1934 the building had deteriorated to the point that the second floor could no longer be used for basketball games and dances. The Wilcoxes constructed a brick theater building on the other side of the town center cemetery and moved the movie operation there in 1938. But for close to 20 years the old Snow/Wilcox block was home for the Orleans Theatre (note the continental spelling of theater), a magic place for Outer Cape Codders, young and old.

The ticket office was right on Main St. After buying a ticket, the movie goer went through a curtain, the only separation between Main St. and the theatre, into an auditorium holding perhaps 150 seats. John Ullman (for many years the managing editor of *The Cape Codder*) remembers taking a gang of Eastham teenagers to the show in his stripped down Model T Ford, fueled with a mixture of gasoline and kerosene. After leaving his friends off at the entrance he inadvertently maneuvered the car so that the exhaust was belching a black plume of evil-smelling fumes directly into the theatre. The curtain offered minimal resistance to the fumes and the audience cleared the theatre in record time.

THE FAMILY INSTALLED THE FIRST AIR CONDITIONING ON THE OUTER CAPE. ON A HOT SUMMER EVENING SPACE UNDER THE STAGE WAS FILLED WITH ICE AND A FAN TURNED ON BEFORE THE PERFORMANCE TO BLOW COOLED AIR INTO THE AUDITORIUM.

Inside, the screen was positioned high up over a stage and those unlucky enough to arrive late and sit up front ended the evening with a semi-permanent crick in the neck. There was always a large bouquet of fresh flowers on each side of the stage and a red velvet curtain covered the screen mounted above. The family installed the first air conditioning on the Outer Cape. On a hot summer evening space under the stage was filled with ice and a fan turned on before the performance to blow cooled air into the auditorium. There were no ushers; you had to find your own seat. Teenaged couples went early to secure sets in the last row so that their romantic activities would escape surveillance by adults.

At first the shows were run three days a week – Wednesday, Friday and Saturday nights, with a matinee on Saturday afternoon (no Sunday movies). Matinee films usually featured cliff hangers such as The Perils of Pauline with the heroine left in a life ending posture only to be rescued and face further dangers in next week's installment. One of these serials' actresses was immortalized in a ditty we sang ad nauseum.

> Shave and a haircut, two-bits.
> Who's in the valley? Tom Mix.
> Who's his girl friend?
> Pearl White!

Chris also booked live entertainment – singers, dancers, magicians, comedians and an occasional minstrel show – in place of movies or on non-movie nights. On a slow night he might walk across Main Street to chat with Bill Higgins who operated a bowling alley and candy store or Dr. Besse, a dentist who also owned many of the store buildings on Main Street. Sometimes Chris would bargain with them and sell the rights to the evening take for, say $10. He would be guaranteed $10 and if the audience was larger than the agreed upon evening's rights the buyer profited. On Saturday afternoons he frequently issued tickets to children that were good for an ice cream cone at Bill Higgins's store. During the Depression years of the early thirties the Orleans Theatre, like most movie houses, gave dishes or glasses to ticket holders to encourage attendance.

Orleans Theatre truck advertising Marlene Dietrich in Blonde Venus.

The Wilcoxes went to Boston once a week to book the movies. The movie owners auctioned the weekly, regional rights to the films. The first-run shows with top stars got top dollars and Chris along with his son Charlie had to bid against movie theater managers in Chatham and Harwich. A typical evening show would have a preview of coming attractions, a Movie tone News Reel, a comedy short and then the feature presentation. Later, a Walt Disney Mickey Mouse or Pluto the Dog short might replace the comedy reel. Double features on Saturday night wold have a B-rated movie followed by the A-rated, feature movie.

The Wilcoxes ran modest ads in the *New Bedford Standard Times* (predecessor of the present *Cape Cod Times*), but word of mouth and posters on the outside of the Snow building or on a truck were probably the more effective ways of attracting customers. The truck cruised around the Outer Cape streets, frequently driven by one of the Wilcox children, adorned with the colorful posters given out by the film marketers. These posters are now considered valuable collectibles, as viewers of the "Antique Roadshow" know. Christine's son, Lloyd Williams, is the proud owner of a poster in good condition featuring, and signed by, Charlton Heston.

Many of the Wilcox family members worked in the Theatre. The oldest son, Charlie, ran the projector, accompanied his father in dealing with the movie rights sales people and eventually became the owner of the business. Mother Bertha and the older girls sold tickets and the youngest, Christine, in her teens, operated a candy concession in the lobby of the new, brick theatre building. She went to wholesalers in Hyannis to buy the candy, priced it and staffed the little candy stand. She reports that she made a profit too.

Mr. and Mrs. Wilcox gave life-time passes to some of their closest friends. Eastham residents Ommund and Edna Howes were one such lucky couple and their son Whit, one of my close childhood friends, saw all of the new movies. My family was not similarly blessed and in any case our parents were too busy and probably too tired in the evening to be interested in the shows. The Theatre was five miles from our home and so my brothers and I rarely saw a movie until the oldest of us four boys, Wilbur, got his license.

By the time I was able to go to the movies, sound had been introduced and I missed the silent movie era, before 1928 – 29, when a piano player supplied mood music or accompanied the action with the appropriate tunes. Both Mary and Christine Wilcox remembered a number of the Theatre's piano players including Eastham's Selma Rongner, Marion Nickerson from Orleans and a Chatham resident, Carl Anderson.

In those days my tastes ran to low comedy or action-packed Westerns. Movies with comedians such as Harold Lloyd, the Marx Brother or Buster Keaton and Westerns featuring Tom Mix, Hoot Gibson or Buck Jones were my special favorites. Burned into my memory are images of the four brothers crammed into a tiny, ocean liner stateroom along with at least 25 other people and more arriving by the second. Not even the boring (we thought), interminable Harpo Marx harp solo in every one of his movies discouraged us from going back for the next Marx Brothers movie. Another vivid mental picture has Tom

The new, brick building housing the Orleans Theatre,
now the home of Orleans CVS pharmacy.

Mix striding into a crowded saloon wearing a large white sombrero, his legs encased in bulky, white, sheepskin chaps and clearing the room of the black-hatted villains.

The first movie I saw was not a comedy or Western but rather the Edgar Rice Burroughs classic, *Tarzan the Ape Man*, starring Johnny Weissmuller. After seeing this dazzling adventure film we practiced swinging from wild grape vines hanging in the woods near our house and tried to emulate Tarzan's ululating cry as he swooped down on a jungle vine, swept Maureen O'Sullivan into his arms and carried her to his tree nest. They just don't make movies like that any more.

TV changed everything for movie houses across the country and the Orleans Theatre was no exception. Charlie Wilcox bought the business from his parents and a while later sold to a conglomerate with theaters all over New England. The new owners operated it for a few years and finally, succumbing to the multi-movie theater trend, closed its doors in the middle 1980s. Years later, walking late at night past the old cemetery on Main St., I sometimes catch a faint, barely audible sound, on some occasions the haunting, male vibrato, Tarzan scream; on others the evocative clippity-clop of Tom Mix's horse, Tony, as the cowboy and his mount disappear into the sunset.

At those times I also become nostalgic for the pre-war, Will Hays, Hollywood Morals Code days, before sex became a spectator sport. A couple had to be married to appear together in bed, both had to be fully clothed in opaque night time attire and the wife had to keep one foot on the floor at all times. The actual consummation of the marriage was never shown, not as today in vivid detail, but only suggested, off-camera. A good example is the 1934 movie, *It Happened One Night*, with Clark Gable and Claudette Colbert. Early in their tempestuous courtship they were forced to spend the night together in a one-room cabin and the plot required that Clark hang a blanket in the middle of the room, between the two beds. Before bedtime there was talk of Jericho's walls falling when Joshua's trumpet sounded – considered pretty racy in those days. At movie's end they finally realized it was true love and when they retired to a motel cabin on their wedding night the camera homed in on the cabin door, a trumpet blared, the background music swelled and THE END appeared on the screen. We all knew, or could imagine, exactly what was happening.

The director of *The Awful Truth* with Cary Grant and Irene Dunne, found another clever way of suggesting rather than showing bedroom activities and also circumventing the Hays code. The 1937 movie portrayed a married couple who had divorced and then began to regret their decision to part. Toward the end of the show, they are together and alone in a house, occupying separate but adjoining bedrooms and their divorce becomes final at midnight. Miss Dunne's room had a clock with two figures, a man and a woman, who on the hour emerge through separate doors, strike the hour by hitting a gong with little hammers and then retire to their respective rooms.

The divorcing couple spend the evening trying to get the door separating their bedrooms to swing open, Miss Dunne's cat insists on napping in front of the door and holds the door shut even when Grant opens his window wide and a heavy breeze blows the curtains almost horizontally. Finally, at midnight the cat is persuaded to move and the door swings open. The camera pans to the clock as the two figures emerge, strike twelve and then the man follows the woman back to her domicile. The music reaches a crescendo and – THE END. We realize that they are getting together but, horrors, they are no longer wed. The director has succeeded in evading the Hays Office rule against unmarried couples being alone, unchaperoned and in bed together. Call me old fashioned but I long for the movies that suggest rather than overwhelming the audience with every graphic detail.

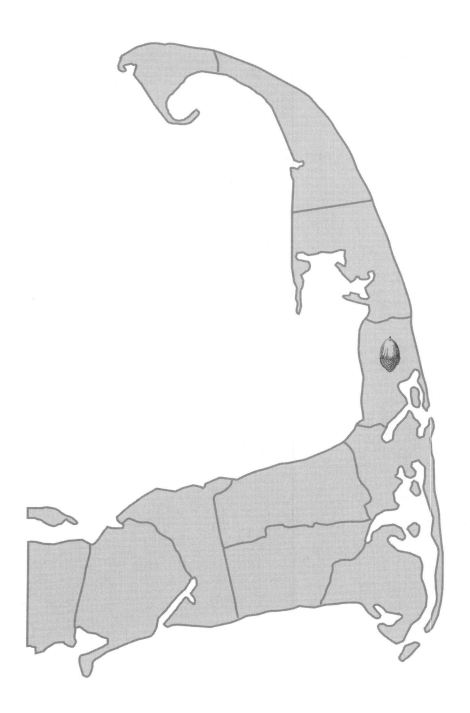

CHAPTER 25

A Texas Size Back Yard

I live in Eastham now, in a house built for my mother when she sold the family homestead in 1959. It is on Nauset Road, within the National Seashore boundaries and so I claim that my back yard contains 69 square miles. Of course I have to share it with the roughly 600 other Outer Cape residents who are lucky enough to own developed land which was within the Cape Cod National Seashore boundaries when the bill establishing the 44,000 acre seashore was filed in 1959. Most of us are quite pleased with our extensive backyards.

This was certainly not the sentiment when the early sponsors of a Cape Cod park – U.S. Representatives O'Neill, Boland and Philbin – filed the first bills in 1957. Its provisions froze building and commercial development in 44,000 acres of proposed park land in the six towns of the outer Cape – Provincetown, Truro, Wellfleet, Eastham, Orleans and Chatham. The acreage included thirty miles of Atlantic Ocean Beach, Chatham to Provincetown, extending various distances westward toward Cape Cod

Bay, in some places as far as the water line. The post-World War II boom had just started and contractors, real estate agents, merchants and other businessmen were infuriated. The establishment of a park would prohibit development of the choicest real estate.

Home owners within the boundaries had different concerns. Most had lived there all their lives and, in Eastham, some traced their ancestry back to the seven "first-comer" settlers in 1644. Under the original bill these home owners would be granted a 25-year suspension of condemnation but all would eventually have to sell to the Government. My family joined the chorus of outraged objectors. Even though our ancestor, Richard Sparrow, was a "late-comer" (he had moved from Plymouth to Eastham in 1653 two years after the "first-comers" arrived), his descendants had lived in Eastham continuously since then and we liked living here.

Public meetings in the various towns, with Government officials presiding and defending the proposal, were contentious. At an Eastham meeting the Park Service Director, Conrad Worth, was accused of promoting Communist ideology. The following evening at a Chatham public meeting a parking attendant said, not recognizing Mr. Worth, "You'd better hurry because they're going to give that guy hell." Representative O'Neill's assistant, Leo Diehl, reported that some Cape Codders burned Boland and O'Neill in effigy. The most creative objections were raised by Chatham Selectman McNeece, who was concerned that "The unspoiled little fishing village would be damaged as a result of the traffic that might be directed towards it."

The bill was stalled in Congress until two U.S. Senators who had ties to the Cape, Kennedy and Saltonstall, joined the bill's supporters. One of Saltonstall's aides, David Martin, recognized that the home owners' distaste for the Government right of eminent domain provision and the prospect of eventually having to sell to the Government was the major sticking point. He came up with a brilliant idea: those whose property had been improved prior to the bill's filing date would be allowed to retain ownership and, with minor exceptions, treat their property the same as any holdings outside the Seashore. This defused what had become an explosive issue and opposition declined.

Discussions about the precise location of boundaries and fine tuning other provisions continued for another two years. During the fine tuning, the word "Seashore" replaced "Park" because hunting was to be allowed and this sport is banned in all Federal Parks. John F. Kennedy, a strong supporter of the bill, was elected President in 1960 and when he was sworn in the following January he pushed it along. Finally, the bill which had been filed on September 3, 1959, was approved by both houses of Congress, signed by Kennedy on August 7, 1961, and the Cape Cod National Seashore became a reality.

The September 3, 1959, filing date was an important, even critical, one for many people. My mother, for example, had just sold the family homestead house and commissioned my builder brother to construct a new house for her on a nearby lot, still within the seashore boundaries. The building permit is dated August 1, 1959. When I took over ownership in 1967 the first thing I did was to apply for, and was granted, a piece of paper I keep in a safe deposit box, a certificate of suspension of condemnation signed by the Superintendent of the Cape Cod National Seashore.

Houses built after the bill was signed were subject to condemnation and purchase at fair market value. Those owners could sell and continue to live in their house under a 25-year lease and many accepted that option. A number of owners took a chance and improved their properties between the date of the bill signing and its passage because they were uncertain as to its future – would it pass or not, or might it be altered prior to final acceptance by Congress? The fate of such "in limbo" properties created major headaches for Seashore administrators but reasonable people can be reasonable and all such cases have been resolved satisfactorily.

Now, 40 years after its establishment, there is still some opposition to the Seashore. Those with special interests: nude bathing beach afficionados, ORV drivers who want access to the beach and sand dunes, builders of trophy houses with a creative interpretation of the regulations and the ones who display bumper stickers saying "Piping Plover Taste Like Chicken." Then there are the die-hards who don't trust the Government. "Yes, it's great now but wait until the next administration changes the rules." Or the rugged individuals who just don't want anyone telling them what to do. "Remember, my ancestors were Mooncussers."

No one pretends that there are no problems. Administration of the Seashore is a complex and daunting task – maintaining visitor facilities and extensive walking or bicycle trails, and providing a multitude of services including nature walks, interpretive lectures, parking, sanitation, lifeguards, and educational programs for about six million visitors a year – mostly during the three summer months. To me, an equally arduous job is dealing with the Interior Department bureaucracy and the Congress of the United States.

Also, administration of a high-turnover staff of professionals and volunteers must be a big headache, especially those with an "us vs. them" mind set. This attitude was particularly prevalent in the early days of the Seashore. In 1967, the first year of my ownership of our house on Nauset Road, a Ranger lived next door in a government-owned house. We became a little irritated over his close and constant monitoring of our activities, calling on us for an inspection when he heard unusual noises like hammering or wood splitting. On one occasion my son mowed a few feet into the Government side of our boundary and the ranger called to make it clear that mowing had to stop at the line.

However, it ended pleasantly when he called to apologize for picking beach plums on our property and gave us a jar of the jelly his wife had made. They had inadvertently stripped our beach plum bushes while we were away and the neighbors had told us, and apparently him, of the infringement upon our shrubs. He was transferred shortly after and our only contact with all succeeding Rangers has been a friendly wave as they drive past the house – with one exception.

My wife and I had been disposing of garden clippings by scattering them in a Seashore pine and oak forestland adjacent to our grounds.

One afternoon a Seashore Ranger appeared at our front door; six feet six inches tall, Marine crew cut, full uniform, holstered gun on one hip and billy club on the other. He explained that his superior had asked him to tell us that it was illegal to discard anything on Government property. We protested, saying that we were actually improving the soil with this good compost and also, Seashore personnel had recently left unsightly piles of chipped pine tree residues right in front of us on Nauset Road. Our words fell on deaf ears. It was made clear that the law is the law. He would not "write us up this time," but we must cease and desist from this practice.

Despite this encounter, unusual I like to think, I would not want to live in Eastham without the Seashore. Most residents concur, including those on the 115 "improved" properties within Eastham's Seashore boundaries. A part of Eastham that I grew up in – where I roamed the fields and woodlands, swam and fished in the ponds, camped and built bonfires on the beaches, cut asparagus and pulled turnips – is preserved, largely unspoiled.

Who says you can't go home again?

POSTSCRIPT

All four of the Sparrow boys, my three brothers and I, left home and the Cape as soon as we were able; we couldn't wait to get away. Wilbur and Robert were drafted into the army in 1940. Wilbur served as a Staff Sargent in Europe with Patton's army and then worked as a builder in Eastham until he suffered a heart attack and died in 1962. Robert transferred to the air force, became a B-24 bomber pilot and was lost when his plane was hit by anti-aircraft fire over Hanover, Germany on his 18th mission in 1944. Fenton enlisted in the air force, flew fighter planes in the U.S. during the war, graduated from Stevens Institute and worked in production for Bethlehem Steel until he retired in 1980. I graduated from Exeter Academy in 1939, from Harvard University in 1943 and worked in a variety of war-related jobs. In 1949 I received a master's degree from M.I.T. and then worked in the Forest Products industry, mostly with the consulting firm Arthur D. Little, until I retired in 1981.

The Cape Cod that we were so anxious to leave looked better and better as we grew older and after working for 40 years in industry Fenton and I returned home, to Orleans and Eastham, respectively. Neither of us have regretted this decision. We have pursued different retirement paths – Fenton went the golf, gardening and shellfishing route while I became heavily involved in town volunteer and elective service. We visit a lot, enjoy each others company and occasionally our spare-time interests overlap as the following illustrates.

Living Off the Land

*T*he more difficult the task the more enjoyable the fruits of the labor. I console myself with this truism as I prepare for a November oystering expedition to Indian Neck in Wellfleet with Fenton. Forecast conditions are for an unusually low tide (minus 2.0 feet), sunrise at 6:45, cloudy and cold with a light drizzle. We will have 90 minutes on the flats, adequate light with the weather dreadful, hopefully, bad enough to discourage even the most hardy of our competition.

As Fenton arrives to pick me up, I am already in my basic winter oystering costume – ancient, green, foam-insulated coveralls – torn and greasy but still serviceable. From an old leather belt hangs an essential article, a three-inch diameter iron ring. Any oyster which can be maneuvered so as to resist falling through the ring is legal, a "keeper."

Into the car trunk goes my green hip boots, a ten-quart bucket with a plastic cola bottle float attached to the handle, heavy wool socks, windbreaker, hat, thermal-lined gloves and of course a long-handled rake. The hat is brown sealskin and equipped with ear flaps. It used to be my best winter headgear and was reserved for dress occasions, but patches of the hair have worn off and now as much leather as fur is exposed.

Fenton is similarly equipped, except that he sports an ancient, mustard-colored, tweed coat with a large fur collar and a stocking cap pulled down to his eyebrows. When preparing for the flats, he pulls over the coat a ragged, blue ski parka. In our full costumes the overall impact is one of seedy, damn-the-world elegance sometimes seen in the skid row area of large cities.

The car is loaded quickly, and we are off to Indian Neck. The tide is still a little high so we sit in the car for a few minutes and

> THE OVERALL IMPACT IS ONE OF SEEDY, DAMN-THE-WORLD ELEGANCE SOMETIMES SEEN IN THE SKID ROW AREA OF LARGE CITIES.

watch the seagulls wheeling overhead. They have beaten us to the flats and are flying over the parking strip macadam to drop their oysters and break the shells. One seems to have a problem and takes off for a second drop. It occurs to us that we can start to fill our buckets early. After the second pass I go out and snatch up the oyster. Attached seaweed cushions the oyster and protects the shell. The second drop had been partly successful; one end of the oyster shell is cracked. I decide not to dispute the gull's claim and throw the oyster back to the pavement. He swiftly swoops in, picks it up, gives me a hard, beady-eyed stare and goes off to find another spot for his next drop.

The tide is finally low enough so we get into our gear and lumber off to the flats. Oystering on foot requires no great skill – just patience, persistence and stamina. A few years ago we could easily fill our bucket on a tide. Now the both of us must work the whole tide to get one bucket between us.

The oysters lie on the surface, partially covered with a thin layer of sand or muck. If there were only live oysters on the flat, it would be relatively simple; but, unfortunately, for every intact oyster there are hundreds of empty oyster and quahog shells, rocks and other inanimate, oyster-like objects. The oysters grow in all sorts of configurations and on almost any solid and stable thing. Pursuing a statistical strategy, we turn

Brothers Donald and Fenton,
when not quahoging.

over everything and start to fill our collection bags. However, the ratio of keepers to throwaways is approaching the point where we don't have the time to turn over enough to fill both buckets on the tide.

The weatherman's prediction is accurate – close to freezing and cloudy with a persistent, heavy mist. We accelerate our normally brisk pace, trying to keep warm and also to fill our buckets and cut short our exposure to the inescapable drizzle. Under such conditions our judgment as to the size of an oyster becomes a bit flawed. We never use the three-inch ring. If there is a question, we would rather not know. We never take illegal ones – only questionable ones, although sometimes only a blind man would find them questionable. We salve our conscience by noting that the seagulls are busy taking oysters and "they don't have any rings," or judging by the empty shells they are going to die anyway, or the law allows 10 percent to be undersize. I hope I never have to defend this position to the Shellfish Warden. At times I am convinced that a predator snail or crab has gotten to the oyster only five minutes before I pick up its empty shell. As we continue to bring up non-oyster objects we curse a perfidious Mother Nature who permits stones to be shaped exactly like oysters.

The tide turns and we agree to collect our oyster buckets and head for dry land. We empty the collection bags into one bucket and it is only slightly rounded, 50 percent below the allowable limit of one ten-quart bucket per person. Rake handles are slipped through the wire loop on the bucket so we can share the load. As we proceed toward dryland we continue to spot oyster-like objects. Not able to bend over, we try to turn them over with our boots to determine if it is an oyster or (almost always) just another rock, single oyster shell, bit of seaweed, etc. We slowly make our crab-like way to the shore, taking turns at kicking away at likely objects and just barely keeping ahead of the tide.

With our gear and precious ten quarts of oysters in the trunk, the ride back to Eastham is a quiet one. It's good to sink into the relative luxury of the car seats and feel the warmth from the car heater.

Back at my house, we dump the oysters on the lawn and divide them, 46 for each of us. Fenton reports that this is about average for a bucket. I ask how many he had gathered this year and without hesitation he says, "It's not been a good year, only 2,328." He is a counter and keeps a log of his harvest from the sea as well as his garden. If in May, I ask how many asparagus stalks he has cut this year, he might reply, "It's early in the season, 262, but that's 27 ahead of last year." It's a holdover from his 30 years in production at Bethlehem Steel when he and his crews were handsomely rewarded when they set records.

Fenton departs and I face up to the hard work of cleaning and opening my oysters. The shells have very sharp projections and some sort of protection is essential when opening the oysters. I have found that a white cotton glove on the left hand eliminates cuts. The glove soaks up oyster juice and quickly gets sloppy. Some observers note critically that I am losing all that good stuff. I tell them, "It's OK, I wring out the glove into the opened oysters when I'm done." Those with no sense of humor find their appetite somewhat diminished. It serves them right – all the more for me.

I prefer my oysters cooked but can't resist eating a few as they are opened, especially the "questionables" that we call "slurpers." Right out of the bay, still ice cold and bathed in salt juice they go down very nicely. Plans are made for an oyster stew for lunch, simplicity is the rule – oysters "plumped out" by heating briefly in their liquor and then into hot milk seasoned with pepper with a good chunk of melting butter. Recently, my wife has been adding a pinch or so of dill weed and I recommend this. The stew should be accompanied by crackers, (Saltines or

Don and Gen Sparrow at his eightieth birthday party.

Pilot according to taste), and have enough oysters so that we don't end up chasing one oyster through a quart of hot milk. Ten or twelve per serving is about right.

We finish the remainder at dinner with Oysters Baltimore. This dish is elegant but easy to make – simmer the oysters briefly in their juice with a little added lemon juice and white wine and then pour the

mixture over a slice of fried ham on buttered toast. A suitable vegetable is frozen asparagus from our spring garden. Thaw, steam, add liberal quantities of butter, season with salt and pepper and serve. As we sop up the juice from our Oysters Baltimore, we comment on how pleasant it is to be retired to Cape Cod, away from the stresses of city life, enjoying the simple life, and eating off the land and sea.

Bibliography

Allen, Everett S. *The Black Ships*. Little Brown and Company, Boston, 1965.

Clark, Col. Eugene S. *Eastham Celebrities*. Audio Tape, Eastham Historical Society, Eastham, Mass., 1963.

Darling, Warren S. *Quahoging Out of Rock Harbor*. Privately printed, Orleans, 1984.

Lincoln, Joseph C. *Cape Cod Yesterdays*. Blue Ribbon Books, Inc., New York, 1935.

Lowe, Alice A. *Nauset on Cape Cod, A History of Eastham*. Eastham Historical Society, 1968.

Pratt, Rev. Enoch, *A Comprehensive History of Eastham, Wellfleet and Orleans*. W. S. Fisher and Co., Yarmouth, Mass., 1844.

Quinn, William P. *The Saltworks of Historic Cape Cod*, Parnassus Imprints, Orleans, Mass., 1993.

Trayser, Donald G. *Eastham, Massachusetts 1651 – 1951*. Eastham Tercentenary, 1951.

Sources of Photos

From the author's files, with the exception of:

Everett Allen, *The Black Ships*
    Chapter 15 - Rumrunner Boat

Glen Boyd
    Chapter 14 - Charlie Escobar

H. K. Cummings, courtesy of William Quinn
    Chapter 11 & 12 - All

Eastham Historical Society
    Chapter 1 - Captain Freeman Hatch, the *Northern Light*
    Chapter 2 - The Three Sisters Lighthouses
    Chapter 5 - All
    Chapter 6 - All
    Chapter 9 - Eastham Town Pump
    Chapter 10 - Sam Brackett's Store and House, George Wiley with wagon
    Chapter 13 - All

Barry Holman and Stephen Grigas
    Front cover - Depot with arriving passengers
    Chapter 7 - Eastham Depot, Depot with arriving passengers

Alice Lowe, *Nauset on Cape Cod*
    Chapter 4 - Eastham's Cable Station and French Cable Station Crew

William Quinn, *Saltworks of Cape Cod*
    Chapter 3 - Dennis saltworks, location of Eastham Saltworks

Quincy Adams Shaw
    Chapter 20 - All

Mrs. Christine Williams
    Chapter 24 - All